Desire and Other Plays

David Lan, born in South Africa in 1952, has lived in London since the age of twenty.

Apart from the plays collected here he has written *Bird Child*, first performed at the Royal Court Theatre Upstairs, two short works, *Painting a Wall* and *Red Earth*, *Flight*, first performed by the Royal Shakespeare Company, and *A Mouthful of Birds*, a collaboration with Caryl Churchill for the Joint Stock Theatre Company. His English version of *Ghetto* by Joshua Sobol was presented by the National Theatre. He received the John Whiting Award in 1977 and the George Orwell Memorial Award in 1983.

After two years of field research in 1980–82 he was awarded a doctorate in Social Anthropology by the London School of Economics. His ethnography, *Guns and Rain: Guerrillas and Spirit Mediums in Zimbabwe*, is taught in universities in Britain, Europe and the United States.

Among his screenplays are three films for the BBC which deal with the effect of contemporary politics in southern Africa on ordinary people: *The Sunday Judge*, set in Mozambique, *Welcome Home Comrades*, set in Namibia; and *Dark City*, set in South Africa. He also co-wrote *Streets of Yesterday*, a political thriller set in Jerusalem and Berlin, for Channel Four.

DESIRE
AND
OTHER PLAYS

DAVID LAN

faber and faber
LONDON · BOSTON

First published in 1990
by Faber and Faber Limited
3 Queen Square London WC1N 3AU

Sergeant Ola was first published in a slightly different version by
Methuen in 1980.

Photoset by Parker Typesetting Service Leicester
Printed in Great Britain by Richard Clay Ltd Bungay Suffolk

© David Lan, 1990
David Lan is hereby identified as author of this
work in accordance with Section 77 of the Copyright,
Designs and Patents Act 1988.

British Library Cataloguing in Publication Data is available

ISBN 0-571-14368-7

CONTENTS

INTRODUCTION

Worlds within Worlds

*Present in every human being are two desires, a desire to know
the truth about the primary world, the given world outside ourselves in
which we are born, live, love, hate and die, and the desire to make
new secondary worlds of our own.*

W. H. Auden

In 1980 I was living in a small mud hut in the vast valley formed
by the Zambezi River as it runs across the extreme north of
Zimbabwe.

To most Zimbabweans the Zambezi Valley is unknown
territory, too dry for commercial farming, so humid no one who
wasn't born there lives there out of choice. The dense bush that
springs up every year after the rains is perfect cover for guerrillas.
Here, fifteen years earlier, the war that ended with the
transformation of Rhodesia into Zimbabwe had begun.

I came to the valley a few months after the war as a social
anthropologist. I wanted to study the relationship that had
developed between the guerrillas and the people of the Valley.
Had the guerrillas won the people's voluntary support, had they
actually lived among them as 'fish in the sea' as the Maoist
textbooks said they should? Or had it been a relationship based on
intimidation, harassment, fear?

I spent two years trying to find out. During those years, apart
from friends who visited me, I was the only so-called white person
for miles around. Almost the only experience of whites most
people in the Valley had had was of soldiers or police. That I
might be a different sort of white was suggested, I think, by the
fact that I lived with a local family in a hut, that I learnt to speak
Shona, the language of the place, and that I spent months
working in the fields with a hoe, a tool rarely seen in white hands.

What I was doing was 'participant observation', the technique social anthropologists use in their attempt to understand other people's lives from their points of view.

Over time it came to be seen that not only was I no especial danger but that my presence in the Valley might even do some good. The first harvest since the war had not yet ripened. All stocks of food had been destroyed by the Rhodesian army and the promises of rations made by the new government had not yet been fulfilled. At night herds of elephants, as hungry as the peasants, trampled through the fields, destroying what they did not eat of the still green maize. The chairman of the local party branch came to see me: Would I take a message to the local council office and tell them how they, my friends, were suffering?

Many similar problems, affecting individuals or the village as a whole, provided ways by which I could repay a little of the generosity I received. One of the first individuals to knock at my door and ask for help was the man whom I've called Jericho in *Desire*.

'Jericho' wanted a loan. During the war he had taken up with and looked after a young girl, Rosemary, who had fled her father's home. When the war was over he began the process of marrying her, paying brideprice as all Shona men do. A few months later when Rosemary became ill she returned to her family. After a while she recovered. Even so, her father (I've called him Kindo), glad to have her back, refused to allow her to return to her husband until Jericho paid yet more brideprice for her.

Like me, Jericho was a stranger to the Valley. He'd arrived during the war to work for the government as one of the attendants at the 'flygate', the barrier at which vehicles coming and going from the Valley are sprayed to kill the tsetse flies that spread sleeping sickness. Almost uniquely in the village, Jericho had an income. Kindo, a courageous supporter of the guerrillas, had lost everything. As much as Jericho had paid him, Kindo wanted more.

Village gossip insisted that more than simply finance fuelled this imbroglio. What was the real reason Kindo couldn't bear to part with the oldest and most beautiful of his daughters? Because he had worked for the government all through the war, Jericho was regarded as a sellout. Why shouldn't Kindo squeeze him? Who could be certain that he really loved his wife? It was known that at his father's house outside the Valley he had a large maize field with knee-high weeds. Was it simply for her labour power he wanted Rosemary?

Whatever the rumours, what was real was that Rosemary had fallen ill again. Jericho was desperate to get her home. The only way was to call Kindo's bluff and pay him the money he demanded. So Jericho came to borrow some from me.

Over the years I was drawn ever deeper into the story of Rosemary and her recurrent illness, which no one could explain. I was there when her 'spirit' or *mudzimu* possessed her and talked to her family about why it had made her ill. In fact the 'real' Rosemary's *mudzimu* was not the guerrilla known as Freedom in the play. The story of Freedom and her bicycle did occur, but in another village and to another family. In the play I've combined a number of families and incidents to tell my version of what seemed to me to be going on in that part of the country when I was there.

Perhaps the key difference between writing 'science', even social science, and writing a play, is that to do the first you need to justify to your colleagues the way you choose to arrange and interpret the data you use; in doing the second you can treat them as you please. In writing all three of the plays in this book I've adapted and altered the original stories that they're based on. At the same time, in terms of the background, social context, history and so on, I've tried to provide a reliable, even an anthropological account of 'how things really are'.

The first two plays were written ten years ago. Reading them now I seem to have done something else as well. Perhaps all explorations of 'the other' in place, in culture, in time, turn out – if they are thorough enough – to be journeys into whomever is doing the exploring at the same time.

In 1976, the Royal Court commissioned a play from me. I wrote *The Winter Dancers* which is set on the north-west coast of Canada among the Kwakiutl Indians. When she finished reading it, my agent of the time sent me a note inviting me to 'come in and explain why you chose this rather remote subject'.

I found it hard to answer her. I had worked in the theatre since the age of fourteen as stage hand, scene painter, puppeteer. I trained as an actor before I'd ever heard of anthropology. If I find a subject interesting, my first thought is: will it make a play? But why this subject had seemed more right than any other I couldn't then (I was twenty-four) even begin to explain. The best I could do was make a case along these lines: Three-thousand-year-old plays are performed from time to time. Leaving the skills of the respective writers to one side, is the world of classical Greece so much closer to our own than the one in which the Kwakiutl live? Or is it only that the Greeks, however long dead, seem more like 'us' than native Americans of a hundred years ago?

I had found the story that became *The Winter Dancers* in an essay by Claude Lévi-Strauss. In *The Sorcerer and his Magic*, Lévi-Strauss analyses a 'fragment of autobiography' by a Kwakiutl shaman known as Quesalid. Autobiographies of shamans are rare enough. What makes this one extraordinary is that, although Quesalid's fame as a healer extended over a large part of British Columbia, what he put on record were, first, the techniques he learnt to deceive his patients and, second, his bewilderment when, once he had performed these bogus rituals, his patients got well.

What interests Lévi-Strauss in this case is the psychology of the sorcerer. He concludes that Quesalid's power lay not in any specialized knowledge, true or false, but in the relationship he formed with his community: 'Quesalid did not become a great shaman because he cured his patients, he cured his patients because he had become a great shaman.'

Quesalid's story seemed to have resonance enough to justify a play. One further element persuaded me to write it.

Far from being an isolated, primitive people, the Kwakiutl had for centuries taken part in trading networks that spread halfway round the world. The last scene of *The Winter Dancers* takes place just as the terms of this trade begin to turn against them, just as the 'white man's' demands for land rights and fishing rights become too insistent to withstand. How good a defence can a belief system already fractured by deceit and self-doubt offer against a sustained attack from the outside? This was the second theme I fed into my play.

A 'remote subject'? Maybe. But *The Winter Dancers* is also, I think, the most personal, almost confessional, piece of writing I've yet achieved. Re-reading my version of Quesalid's autobiography now, I seem to have journeyed halfway round the world only to end up by writing my own.

The first performances of *The Winter Dancers* took place in London in 1977. The next year I attended rehearsals for a production in Los Angeles. In the plane on the way home I found I had caught flu. In the feverish state brought on in equal parts by six weeks in the United States and a high temperature it occurred to me, literally out of the blue, that *The Winter Dancers* was only the first play of a cycle of three.

In this one, religion and ritual confront the earliest stages of colonialism. The outlines of two more were suddenly clear to me: in one, ritual and colonialism would be at war with each other; in the last, ritual would help to bring colonialism to an end. I thought the last would be set in Mozambique. I knew the second would take place in New Guinea.

During the Second World War, the United States used New Guinea as an air base. New Guineans with almost no experience of modern technology watched amazed as flocks of aeroplanes landed and disgorged mountains of machinery, clothing, food. Many coastal New Guineans had recently lost land to Australian entrepreneurs and been forced to seek work on foreign-owned copra plantations. They laboured for a pittance, while for the whites who seemed to do no work at all unimaginable wealth fell out of the skies.

The belief grew that the reason the aeroplanes brought cargo to the whites was that they knew and performed certain secret rituals. If New Guineans could discover these rituals, the aeroplanes would bring cargo to them.

Years went by. Ritual after ritual imitating the daily lives of the whites were performed. Cargo failed to come. The original belief, that the benefits of technology could be obtained without labour, was replaced by a more radical one, namely that cargo actually belonged to the native peoples. By persuading them to abandon their own religion in favour of Christianity the whites had cheated the New Guineans out of their own wealth, their own power. If they took back their own land, regained control of their own destinies, cargo would surely come.

In Peter Lawrence's *Road Belong Cargo* I found the story of Yali Singina, the dominant cargo leader of northern New Guinea. With Lawrence's support and advice, I based my leading character largely on him.

The first production of *Sergeant Ola* was in October 1979. About that time I happened to watch a TV documentary about the current state of the civil war in Zimbabwe. Among the people interviewed was a Shona nationalist and historian. Arguing with a member of the Rhodesian government about the extent of support for the rebels in the countryside, he mentioned that among those who collaborated most closely with the guerrillas were spirit mediums.

Six months later I was in Zimbabwe. Five years later I published a book called *Guns and Rain: Guerrillas and Spirit Mediums in Zimbabwe*. Two years after that, ten years after I had realized I was writing a cycle, I at last began to write *Desire*, the third and final play.

What these plays seem to be about is that religion, far from being 'the opium of the people', is actually an unlimited and perpetually fruitful resource. In times of material and spiritual hardship people can draw on it to fuel resistance. Some kinds of religion will be more effective than others. 'Cargo' leads into a brick wall. Perhaps these plays might make you think about Catholicism in Eastern Europe, Buddhism in Tibet, the Anglican church in South Africa or even in modern Britain in a slightly different way.

Writing this in the last days of the 1980s as the governments of Eastern Europe come crashing down, it seems clearer, perhaps, than it has ever been that one of the biggest mistakes politicians of the Left have made in Africa, in Asia and in Europe has been to see religion as the kind of thought 'progress' makes disappear. The one great virtue of the anthropological view of things is that, without eschewing criticism, it takes for granted the need to treat with all possible tenderness and respect how people without power feel and think and dream.

But these plays are not, I hope, lectures with feet. One of the things anthropologists try to do in writing about 'their' people is construct a moral universe within which the lives, the actions and emotions of members of the societies they describe can be understood and evaluated both in the terms they themselves use, and in terms of the world from which the anthropologist came. This is, it seems to me, also what playwrights do. At least, I have tried to do this in writing these plays.

David Lan
London, December 1989

The Winter Dancers

For Byron Foster

CHARACTERS

BETSY HUNT
CARVER, a shaman
ONE FOOT, his sister
KETTLE, his wife
DANCER, his son
MOUNTAIN PEAK, his father
FOOL, Kettle's brother, a dreamer
BLOOD LIP, a shaman
MOUSE, a woman shaman
FOREST, a shaman
WELL WASHED STONE, a shaman
LIFE OWNER, a shaman
SKY, Life Owner's daughter
WHALE, a chief

The play is set on Vancouver Island, off the coast of British Columbia, between autumn 1871 and summer 1891. There is an interval between scenes four and five.

The Winter Dancers was first performed in the Theatre Upstairs at the Royal Court Theatre on 15 June 1977. The cast was as follows:

BETSY HUNT	Betty Hardy
CARVER	Jack Shepherd
FOOL	John McEnery
KETTLE	Mary Larkin
MOUNTAIN PEAK	
FOREST	Alex McCrindle
LIFE OWNER	
ONE FOOT	
MOUSE	Stassia Stakis
SKY	
BLOOD LIP	
WHALE	Fred Pearson
WELL WASHED STONE	
DANCER	Sean Scanlan

Director	Ian Kellgren
Designer	Gillian Daniell
Lighting Designer	Steve Whitson

Autumn 1871.
Very early morning. Soft sounds of birds. The sun rises.
CARVER *is fishing with a short pole from the end of a pier, a large*
European-style kettle at his side. He smacks his lips at the water to
encourage the fish to bite.

CARVER: Now don't you swim about and watch our poor younger
  brother all day long. Go for it, Old Woman. (*Smacks his lips.*)
  Take your sweet sweet sweet sweet food. Take it, Old Man.
  Take it. Take it. Take it.

  (BETSY HUNT, *an old woman, stands to one side.*)

BETSY HUNT: In these days when we Kwakiutl Indians clean
  forget just who we are, some people come together to hold
  our festivals again. The main one is the potlatch. Yes. In old
  days each man had his place. Times were easy then. The sea
  was bursting full of fish. Fish to eat. Fish to sell to traders.
  The chief and the high men would work all year, collect up
  many hundred blankets. Every blanket you lend out, in one
  year two come back. One man would hold a potlatch. We'd
  dance and sing. He'd give his wealth away. Everyone got
  some amount of blankets, each according to his place. And
  then to show how great a man he was, sometimes his house
  would burn, canoe would burn, everything gone, his wealth
  destroyed. And we would say: that whatsisname, oh, he's a
  powerful man.

  My grandfather had a different power. He was the greatest
  shaman in the world. He cured all the people's sickness. He
  sucked the sickness out of them. Oh, he was praised.
  Whenever anyone fell sick, they called my grandfather to
  cure. He danced, and then he sucked the sickness out and
  they were well.

  But we were wild men then. Oh wild. In our festivals our
  boys ate human flesh. No more. Not since the white men
  came. Mr Hart the missionary told me: girl, you're lucky
  that you left that place. You, granddaughter to a man like

5

that. No doubt about it, girl. You'd end your days in hell.
(*Sound of a young girl –* ONE FOOT *– crying, off.*
FOOL *scuttles in, sees* CARVER, *stops running and saunters
forward. He affects a yawn, stretches, looks out over the sea.*)

FOOL: A huge bird's wing. You see it, boy? Across the sea. Grey,
soft, warm.

CARVER: Where've you been? I had to take the nets out by
myself.
(FOOL *picks up a fishing spear and stands with it poised over the
water.*)

FOOL: The air is calm, the cold is calm, the haze is calm –
(*He jabs the spear into the water. Simultaneously* ONE FOOT
cries out again. FOOL *starts, and misses the fish.*)
Missed. Your sister screeched all night so loud I went into
the wood to cool my ears.

CARVER: I blocked my ears with pine gum.
(FOOL *kicks the earth.*)

FOOL: That's you, boy.

CARVER: No. She's been grieving since her husband drowned.
You're on your toes to huddle in her bed. She'll stop her
howling then. So who's the one you went to in the woods,
boy? Is she sweet?
(*A loud calling off. A man's voice,* BLOOD LIP, *intoning in
falsetto, the call of the raven.*)

BLOOD LIP: (*Off*) Kama ka kei. Kama Ka Kei.
(CARVER *looks up.* FOOL *stands watching, alert.* KETTLE *enters
carrying a bowl of steaming water and another containing herbs.
She kneels and mixes a herbal medicine.*)

KETTLE: You'd better come, boy. The only ones who stay away
have got good reason to.

CARVER: Who went to call the shaman? What for? One Foot
won't die.

FOOL: You sure of that?

KETTLE: This head man of his family slept thick as rock through
all his sister's cries. A head man must show sympathy or
what's the use of him?

FOOL: No use. Pitch him in the sea.

CARVER: I've got better than sympathy. I've got understanding.

6

KETTLE: Not now, boy. The shaman's here. You'd better come.
(ONE FOOT, *weeping, comes on supported by her father,*
MOUNTAIN PEAK. *He lays her down.* KETTLE *dips her finger in*
her bowl and holds it to ONE FOOT's *lips.* ONE FOOT *whimpers*
and cries.)
MOUNTAIN PEAK: An enemy spirit. Streaming on the wind.
Across the mountains. Through the trees. Some rival worms
his way inside my daughter's flesh to bring me down.
(*He takes the bowl from* KETTLE *and pours it out.*)
This is past your kitchen remedies.
(MOUNTAIN PEAK, FOOL *and* KETTLE *form a semi-circle*
behind ONE FOOT. *They hold pieces of carved wood which they*
will beat together. CARVER *stands to one side.*
BLOOD LIP *enters and goes directly to* ONE FOOT. *He takes her*
head in his hands. She is immediately quiet and still. He bares
her body to the waist. Throughout the scene he never looks anyone
directly in the face.)

(*The Curing Ceremony:*
FOOL, MOUNTAIN PEAK *and* KETTLE *begin to beat a rhythm*
with the sticks. BLOOD LIP *breathes heavily. The tempo of his*
breathing increases. Then he flips over twice and on to his back.
His body trembles violently, then becomes rigid.
MOUNTAIN PEAK *and* FOOL *lift him up. He runs round in a*
circle. He calls out loud and inarticulate sounds. The running gets
slower. He stands still.)
BLOOD LIP: (*In falsetto*) Oh friends, where have I been and who
has carried me home?
(*He kneels. Soft singing is heard, high pitched and eery. All*
attention is focused on BLOOD LIP *throughout. He feels*
ONE FOOT's *chest and side looking for the site of the illness. He*
finds it. He begins to suck. The air squeaks as it squeezes into his
mouth. The sucks are prolonged and powerful. After the fourth he
opens his mouth and blood drips out. He spits into his hand. The
beating stops. He takes from his hand an object like a fat
wriggling worm and shows it.)
I hold the sickness in my hand. Aiiii!
(*He plunges his hand into the bowl of water, then takes it out and*

throws it open and up. The sickness has vanished. He goes to one side and sits. ONE FOOT *sits up, then stands.* MOUNTAIN PEAK *embraces her. He weeps.*)

MOUNTAIN PEAK: Let me see the sickness. Let me see the evil sent against me.

BLOOD LIP: You saw it writhing on my palm. It's gone. Whipped up by the air.

(ONE FOOT, *still in* MOUNTAIN PEAK's *embrace, sags.* KETTLE *runs to her.*)

KETTLE: Can she rest now?

BLOOD LIP: As she likes. She's cured.

(KETTLE *takes her aside.* FOOL *strokes her hair.* BLOOD LIP *seems to draw information from the air.*)

You were dancing? You were dancing?

(ONE FOOT *nods.*)

MOUNTAIN PEAK: Was that the cause? Dances out of season?

(*He goes back to* ONE FOOT.)

I had a fever once, my fish. My body ran with sweaty streams. I lay, a river in my bed and pissed from every pore. Ha ha ha ha. But you. He drained your river at its source.

(BLOOD LIP's *body goes rigid. His eyes go back in his head. He trembles violently all over. They watch him. His mouth opens and blood pours out. From his tongue he takes a quartz crystal. He pours water over his hand to wash it.*)

BLOOD LIP: Power lies
in the crystal
where it hides
at the seat of the power-man's soul.
Ha!
Where it lies
where it hides
he
that man, great man
loved man, strong man
will have power so bright
will have power so dark
will have power so sharp.
Where I throw it there it lies

Where I throw it there it hides.
Ha!

(*He throws it. It vanishes into the air but is heard bouncing off the roof.* BLOOD LIP *follows its path with his finger. It bounces off the walls. Finally it comes to rest in* CARVER's *stomach.* BLOOD LIP *puts his hands on* CARVER's *shoulders.*)

This one. He. The crystal chooses well. You have power in you, friend. You will be called. Ha! Ten blankets. I must go.

(MOUNTAIN PEAK *places a pile of blankets at* BLOOD LIP's *feet.*)

I take the payment from the father, not the son. Shaman does not take from shaman. Between them all the world is shared.

(*He picks up the blankets and goes out.* MOUNTAIN PEAK *takes* ONE FOOT *out. After a moment* CARVER *takes up his fishing rod and casts his line.*)

CARVER: Ha!

KETTLE: You feel the power, Carver? Do you feel the power? I've got a right to know the man I married.

(*She bares* CARVER's *stomach and feels it to discover where the crystal entered. She finds no hole.*)

Smooth skin. (*To* FOOL) Is that the way?

(CARVER *smacks his lips at the water.*)

All shamans float. If you're a shaman – float!

(CARVER *holds out his hands and tries to rise. Nothing happens. He laughs.*)

You're not a shaman's arsehole!

CARVER: A shaman says I am.

FOOL: Don't smile too wide. Your sister's cured.

CARVER: Look. I send down food for swimmers on my hook. They open wide their jaw and snap – cool treachery. What should bring life brings death. Now, us. Say we forget to do a winter dance. Say I slept on you when you're still full of blood and so to punish us the rain won't fall or deer never come home. We pay out wealth to shamans. But do we ever set our minds to making what's bad better? Now, do these swimmers pay to end their misery? No. By autumn time they've grown so smart they steal the worm clean off my

9

hook and leave it dangling bare. They take their lives in their own hands to turn the evil in this world to good.

KETTLE: But she's cured.

(*She gathers her bowls and herbs together.*)

Just pray you're never ill. You attack them and accuse them so often and so loud no shaman's going to come to care for you.

(FOOL *takes the fishing pole from* CARVER.)

FOOL: Hey hey hey hey!

(*He lands a fish.*)

CARVER: What trick is that?

FOOL: Ha ha ha, Old Man. I'm so glad you could come.

(*He beats the fish on the head with a stick.*)

(*Intoning*) Now, soul. Go back to the deep, bleak places where you live, O giver of fine weight.

KETTLE: You're not a shaman's foreskin, boy.

CARVER: Look. If you want evil spirits I'll drag one from his mouth. Open up. There she is. Pull!

FOOL: Aaahrgh!

CARVER: It's his tongue. I'll pull an evil spirit from his pants.

(*He pulls* FOOL *over and they roll on the ground.* FOOL *laughs.*)

Got her! Kettle! Here's a wriggling worm.

KETTLE: (*With great intensity*) Are you a shaman?

CARVER: Time to get the nets.

(*He takes the fishing pole and spear out.* KETTLE *waits till he has gone then speaks urgently to her brother.*)

KETTLE: Is he a shaman?

FOOL: Take care of him. They'll be after him tonight.

KETTLE: Who will? You've always understood these mysteries. I won't let evil near.

FOOL: Call me. I'll run.

(CARVER *comes in.*)

CARVER: I took the nets out, boy. Come now or you'll drag them in alone.

KETTLE: One Foot kept me up five nights. Now you. No sleep again tonight.

(*She goes out.*)

FOOL: Remember all your dreams. Night speaks with many voices. The strangest are the true.

(*He drops the fish into the kettle and takes it off.*)

CARVER: I am the principal one who says: I don't believe in
shamans. They've heard me say it many times. That's why, I
think, they've chosen me. I'm not the fisherman who says:
You see this little swimmer? The spirits hung him on my
hook. You see this giant oily wopper? I caught him with my
hands. For me it's every fish or none. They've given me the
chance to learn if they are real or if they just pretend. No man
can be a shaman if he doesn't have a dream. If there's no
dream, no special vision for himself alone, he has no power,
clean.
Night came. I blew the candle out. I closed my eyes to sleep. I
waited for a dream. The house grew cold. I slept. But no
dream came. Clear, dreamless, dreamless sleep.
If they come for me I'll go with them to see if they are false or if
they're true. And if I find they're false we'll drive them off our
island. O Great Chief Father Sun. I swear: if I learn truth and
keep it from my people, let me live among dry rocks. Alone.
Unloved. The most deceived. O Great Chief Father Sun.
(*Three shamans enter:* BLOOD LIP, WELL WASHED STONE *and*
FOREST. *They are followed by the dreamer,* FOOL, *and the
shaman woman,* MOUSE. *They are all masked. They sit.*)
This was my dream: I went out hunting seals. I saw a wolf. A
bone stuck crossways in his jaw and very deep. I said: I will
cure you, friend. I tied a rope tight to the bone, pulled on it
and out it came. And then I dreamed a man came and he said:
there is nothing that you wish for you won't have. Then I
woke. And outside it was light.
(*A wolf howls.*)

BLOOD LIP: So you are Carver?
   (CARVER *nods. He is facing* BLOOD LIP *who stares at him.*
   WELL WASHED STONE *does not move when he speaks.*)

WELL WASHED STONE: What can you see?

CARVER: Tunnels. Through his eyes. A tunnel. No. No!
   (*Overcome with fear, he strains to tear away.* BLOOD LIP
   maintains his fixed stare.)

CARVER: Stone.

WELL WASHED STONE: What is that you carve?

WELL WASHED STONE: Bone?

CARVER: Stone. Wood.

WELL WASHED STONE: Blood? What do you see?

CARVER: Nothing. Darkness.

WELL WASHED STONE: Where?

CARVER: Inside his eyes.

WELL WASHED STONE: Wells of darkness? Leading down from darkness into darkness.

CARVER: Yes.

WELL WASHED STONE: From night on into night? And are you flying? Answer!

CARVER: Help me.

(*A wolf howls.* CARVER *faints. As* BLOOD LIP *removes his mask his tone changes from mysterious to practical.*)

BLOOD LIP: He'll choke!

(FOOL *turns* CARVER *on to his side and holds his tongue flat.* MOUSE *splashes water on to* CARVER's *face.* FOOL *lifts* CARVER's *shoulders so his head hangs down between his knees.*)

WELL WASHED STONE: He's coming back.

BLOOD LIP: Arse upwards. Quick.

(FOOL *turns* CARVER *so he lies face downwards.* MOUSE *splashes water on the back of* CARVER's *head.*)
Ready?
(MOUSE *and* FOOL *go back to their places.* CARVER *crawls up into a kneeling position facing away from* BLOOD LIP *who has replaced his mask. The shamans regain their distance and poise.*)
Carver?
(CARVER *turns.*)

WELL WASHED STONE: Your soul is safe in the base of your spine. Now. Answer. Do you wish to brave our wilderness? Or to walk the well-marked path?

CARVER: I have been chosen. If you will teach me I will learn.

(WELL WASHED STONE *takes off his mask. He smiles.*)

WELL WASHED STONE: I am Well Washed Stone, Shaman of the Mamalelakwala. This one, Blood Lip, you know.

(BLOOD LIP *takes off his mask. He smiles.*)
And this one too you know.
(FOOL *takes off his mask.*)

12

CARVER: Fool! Are you a shaman?

FOOL: I am a dreamer.

CARVER: What is a dreamer?

WELL WASHED STONE: Hush. A dreamer is a shaman's second eyes. He listens. And he sees. He knows all the bays and all the inlets. Every village. Every house.

FOOL: I travel up and down the coast. No one knows I am the shamans' second eyes. The people take me in and give me food. I talk and sing with them. I take out fish nets with the men. I press bark cloth with the wives. I find out who is ill. Who is unhappy. Who is pregnant. Lonely. Dying. I see a blister on a mother's breast. I hear bowels squeeze, then whimpering in the dark. When night hides me from spies I paddle home and say what I have seen.

WELL WASHED STONE: Our coming is a mystery. We say: I see your sickness. Yes, they say. And they believe. We know. (FOREST *claps his hands twice.* BLOOD LIP *begins to breathe heavily. The tempo of his breathing increases. Then he flips over twice and on to his back. His body trembles violently and becomes rigid.* FOOL *and* MOUSE *lift him up.* WELL WASHED STONE *whispers*)
See? His soul has leapt out of his spine. You understand my point?
(BLOOD LIP *burps. They all roar with laughter.*)
If you burp or laugh you say: some girlish spirit prances in my mind.
(*They laugh.*)
Some girlish spirit. So. Enough of that.

CARVER: I have heard that shamans –

WELL WASHED STONE: (*Threatening but quickly*) Carver, stranger, boy – you never say what you see here.
(CARVER *shakes his head.*)
Never. Or wander lost in thick night's tangle. No way out before you, no way out behind. Morning Climber.

CARVER: Yes?

WELL WASHED STONE: Where is he?

CARVER: Where?

WELL WASHED STONE: Morning Climber. Did you know him?

13

CARVER: Yes. My sister's husband.

WELL WASHED STONE: Where is he?

CARVER: Dead. He drowned.

WELL WASHED STONE: How, drowned?

CARVER: Great Salmon River. It washed him over rapids.

WELL WASHED STONE: Why?

CARVER: Why?

WELL WASHED STONE: He told.

CARVER: Morning Climber was –

WELL WASHED STONE: He told.

CARVER: You killed him?

WELL WASHED STONE: Killed? Great Salmon River washed him over rapids. So, you must learn with crystal mind and crystal eye. If there's a flaw we can not save you. You are wolf's child. You are wolf's child.

(MOUSE *has fallen asleep.* FOREST *nudges her and she repeats the wolf howl she made previously.*)

He will protect you. But only from the world of evil. Never from yourself. Enough of that.

CARVER: I have heard – that shamans can *cause* sickness. People say that working for his chief he can throw sickness in the flesh of enemies. How is this done?

(*Silence.*)

BLOOD LIP: High in the head of the tallest cedar eagle builds her nest. When her child learns flying he only has one chance. If he falls, his neck breaks on the forest floor. We are not so cruel. Keep both feet firm. Then try a little skip. Then hop. Then jump. In time we'll teach you flying. Sleep now. Sleep now. Sleep.

(CARVER *falls asleep. The shamans go out.*

KETTLE *comes in. She sees* CARVER *and runs to him.*)

KETTLE: Carver.

(*He wakes, pushes her away.*)

Why are you sleeping in the graveyard?

CARVER: Trickery. It's all, all trickery.

(*His leg buckles. He falls. He crawls along the ground and stands awkwardly.*)

I've seen into the sunless pits.

14

(She goes to him. He pushes her away and stands erect.)

They're empty.

(He embraces her tightly.)

KETTLE: Come home.

(She leads him out. Bird-song.)

BETSY HUNT: I went on a train to Michigan. They had a festival of all the Indians there. There wasn't much about us Kwakiutl. Drawings and some masks. Not good ones, no. My father helped some white man write down facts about our people. We read these stories now. We tell our children: see, that's how they lived. The potlatches. The dances. Oh – so many things. The right behaviours. Who to marry. Who is cousin. Who is not. Excepting in the books, it's all lost now. The fish are lost. The trees.

My grandfather Quesalid disappeared the year when I was born. 1891, that was. I don't remember him too well. My father told me, once I stayed with him. Then his wife Kettle cared for me. Our chief at that time was called Fool. This great chief Fool came down from the mountain top one day and told our people: Great Shaman Quesalid has gone into the air. No one understood these words. So Fool says: Fire came down from the sky. Fire carried our shaman off into the clouds. Fool says: our shaman will return one day and drive the white men from our land. That's what Fool said. But I say this: those people thought the world came to an end across the strait. Never listen to a man who's lived his life out on an island. He thinks the island is the world so all the rest must be a savage place. Ha ha ha ha.

But I think: oh, we've had hard times. In our hard times I thought: my father's father was the greatest shaman in the world. And even though they didn't know the world is wider than Vancouver Island, in our winter's night out in the cold, thinking that – it almost kept me warm.

TWO

Autumn 1873.

Heavy rain beats down on the roof. MOUNTAIN PEAK *sits leaning against a big wooden box, an ornately carved rifle on his lap, drinking from a small stone jar.*

FOOL: The Blackfoot chief waited at the far side of the square. Chief Elk stopped in front of me. *You* talk to him, he said.

MOUNTAIN PEAK: And Carver?

FOOL: He stood behind me.

(MOUNTAIN PEAK *drinks*.)

I said: Why me? I thought: they're testing me. Chief Elk said: you're head man of your family. You're number seven in the village. You speak to him.

MOUNTAIN PEAK: And Carver?

FOOL: I said: I've never talked with foreign men before. Carver only gave his place to me last spring. I haven't held a potlatch to confirm it yet.

(CARVER *comes in. He takes a blanket, wet from the rain, off his shoulders*.)

I'm telling him what I said to the Blackfoot chief.

(CARVER *goes out*.)

MOUNTAIN PEAK: My father gave his place to me. His father gave the place to him. His father and his father, his father and his father. I gave it to my son, Carver. He gave the place to you. What about *his* son? Little shrimp. When Carver was born I gave a potlatch so big every person in this village was in my debt. And when *his* son was born? He wouldn't give the snot out of his nose.

FOOL: A shaman doesn't need to win respect by potlatching.

MOUNTAIN PEAK: Carver's not a shaman. Ha ha ha ha.

FOOL: His fame is spreading up and down the coast. A shaman doesn't need a place. His power lies inside.

MOUNTAIN PEAK: Then why didn't he return the place to me? I'm giving you my daughter. Isn't that enough? What kind of power does he have?

FOOL: Power to protect me.

MOUNTAIN PEAK: From who? From Blackfoot chiefs? Ha ha ha ha. What do those brutes want now?

FOOL: Land.

MOUNTAIN PEAK: The Blackfoot own mountains, rivers, plains. I've been there, boy. I've seen. A land ten times this

16

whale's turd.

FOOL: (*Impatiently*) It's gone.

MOUNTAIN PEAK: Gone?

FOOL: Taken.

MOUNTAIN PEAK: Away?

FOOL: Sold.

(*The rain begins to blow away.*)

MOUNTAIN PEAK: Sold. I can sell my left hand, see? How much
will you give me? Fifteen blankets? Done. Put them on my
pile. Now come and take your property. Ha ha.

(*He boxes with his right hand.*)

FOOL: The Blackfoot gave us gifts. Twenty rifles. We gave him
food. I said: this is our land. Our fathers' graves lie here.
You live on open plains. Gallop a horse across our stony
ground. He'll sprawl and crush his bones. The Blackfoot
bowed his head. He took three small paces back. Then
quick as life he drew a dagger from his hair. With two
strokes he opened up his chest. No blood. And then it
spurted through the air. He fell. His fingers tear at rock.
He rises up, cries curses to the sky and reels. His back
struck hard the earth. He lay. His raw heart glistening, wet.
A salmon jerking on a stone. Until it dies.

(*He drinks. The rain has gone.*)

MOUNTAIN PEAK: And Carver?

FOOL: I wouldn't speak a word without him there.

MOUNTAIN PEAK: Give him his place back. You won't need
protection then.

(FOOL *starts sewing buttons on to a blanket using a large
needle.*

CARVER *comes on carrying a child wrapped in a cloth. He sits
playing with his son.*

MOUNTAIN PEAK *points the rifle at* CARVER, *holding it back
to front, peering up the barrel.*)

FOOL: The other way.

MOUNTAIN PEAK: Again?

FOOL: Turn it the other way.

(MOUNTAIN PEAK *turns it upside down.*)

The other way!

(MOUNTAIN PEAK *turns his back on* CARVER, *still peering up the barrel*.)

MOUNTAIN PEAK: I can't see anything now.

(*He throws the rifle down and picks up the stone jar.*

To FOOL) Who gave this gin?

FOOL: Chief Elk. Carver cured his son.

MOUNTAIN PEAK: It's my wife. His mother's blood calling from the grave. What about *your* son, boy? You'll need to do some clever curing there.

(*He drinks.*

CARVER, *still holding his son, starts chipping at a stone with a steel adze.*)

Sew your blankets, Fool. You'll earn a mighty place. You'll pass it to your son. He'll chuck it in a ditch. Little shrimp.

(*He goes out.*

FOOL *looks outside then sits closer to* CARVER.)

FOOL: You must go to the Mamalelakwala, boy.

CARVER: When?

FOOL: Tonight. The great chief's son is dying.

CARVER: I can't miss your potlatch, boy. Find someone else.

FOOL: They'll pay well. Twenty blankets.

CARVER: Chief Elk paid twenty-five. And all this gin.

FOOL: Life Owner tried and failed.

CARVER: There's no hope then.

FOOL: No. Except, he dreamed of you.

CARVER: Who dreamed?

FOOL: The sick boy dreamed a man called Carver came and sucked his sickness.

CARVER: He dreamed of me.

FOOL: Why not? You're famous. They'll all be dreaming of you soon.

CARVER: You didn't set one toe in your canoe all day. How did you find this out?

FOOL: Don't ask, boy. Do your work. Believe.

CARVER: I am a fisherman. My work is with the sea.

FOOL: There's a clear path from the bay to the house. They'll send a son to row you home. He's dying. Will you go, boy? Say.

(FOOL *gestures not to talk*.

KETTLE *and* ONE FOOT *come on carrying baskets*.)

CARVER: Where've you been?

KETTLE: How long has Dancer been in the cold?

CARVER: I keep him warm. Where have you been?

(MOUNTAIN PEAK *comes on*.

ONE FOOT *giggles and covers her mouth*.)

MOUNTAIN PEAK: Don't laugh at me. I'm old. Soft. White.
Flesh like roe. I'm flat out on your plate. Salt me. Gobble me
up. Where's my wife?

(*He drinks*.)

FOOL: The basket's not half full. I won't marry a girl who can't
collect in food.

KETTLE: The trees are bare. This lot's the last.

FOOL: What took so long collecting then?

ONE FOOT: Cheer up, boy. We're glad we're home.

(KETTLE *holds* CARVER's *head in her hands*.)

MOUNTAIN PEAK: Knock knock ringing through my head. Half
their lives on water. Half their lives on rock. No wonder half
our people are half mad. What's she giggling at?

KETTLE: We dance tomorrow. In six days she gets married. She's
excited.

FOOL: She's been married before.

MOUNTAIN PEAK: A pig's life. Knock knock knock.

FOOL: There's dances every year.

MOUNTAIN PEAK: Snuffling in the dirt.

FOOL: We're hungry now.

KETTLE: Then cook the food yourself.

(ONE FOOT *giggles and snorts*.)

MOUNTAIN PEAK: You left our One Foot in the snow. You
brought a sea lion home.

(FOOL *has given* ONE FOOT *a needle and blanket*. CARVER
chips and rocks his son. FOOL *and* ONE FOOT *sew*.

MOUNTAIN PEAK *drinks*. KETTLE *mashes berries by rolling a
stone over them*.)

KETTLE: (*Sings*)

When I am grown I will bend and pick up clams
When I am grown I'll pick berries all day long.

MOUNTAIN PEAK: Stop that knocking or I'll drown myself.

(CARVER *stops chipping.*)

KETTLE: (*Sings*)

> When I am grown I'll catch salmon in my nets.
> When I am grown I'll catch whales and drag them home.

(*They work in silence. After a moment* FOOL *stands and gestures to* CARVER *to come outside with him.*

ONE FOOT *starts the performance of the trick she,* KETTLE *and* MOUNTAIN PEAK *have prepared, by asking her first question and giving the absurd answer as if nothing special were anticipated. As the routine progresses her tone becomes more demanding.* CARVER *and* FOOL *are – and* KETTLE *and* MOUNTAIN PEAK *pretend to be – nonplussed.*)

ONE FOOT: Will someone bring me a knife?

FOOL: What for?

ONE FOOT: To cut my head off.

CARVER: Have you let her drink?

(KETTLE *hands* ONE FOOT *a basket.*)

KETTLE: Start mashing these.

FOOL: She's busy.

(FOOL *gestures to* CARVER *to go outside.*)

ONE FOOT: Will someone bring me a hammer?

KETTLE: They're late fruit but they're not that hard.

CARVER: What do you want a hammer for?

ONE FOOT: To crush my head.

CARVER: She's drunk.

MOUNTAIN PEAK: You bring the gin home, boy.

CARVER: Go start the cooking.

ONE FOOT: Will someone bring me a paddle to chop my head in two?

KETTLE: Stop now or your brother will punish you.

ONE FOOT: Will someone bring me a box to hide myself?

(MOUNTAIN PEAK *lifts up the box he has been leaning against.*)

MOUNTAIN PEAK: All right, treasure. Hide yourself in this.

KETTLE: I told her not to go on.

(MOUNTAIN PEAK *opens the door of the box.*)

ONE FOOT: I'm hiding myself inside this box.

(*She gets in and closes the door.*)

FOOL: What's happening? Carver? What's she doing?

CARVER: Come out of there.

KETTLE: I warned you. You'll be punished.

> (*She picks up a heavy mallet.*)

> You're a wicked girl. You don't do what you're told. I'll punish you for that.

> (*She lifts the mallet above her head and is about to bring it down on the box.* CARVER *dashes forward and grabs* KETTLE's *arm.* FOOL *takes hold of the mallet.*)

CARVER: Are you mad? You'll kill her.

> (MOUNTAIN PEAK *and* KETTLE *burst out laughing.* CARVER *and* FOOL *are amazed.* MOUNTAIN PEAK *opens the box and shows that it is empty.*)

ONE FOOT: (*Off*) I'm coming. I'm coming. I'm coming. I'm here.

> (*She runs on laughing and flings her arms round* FOOL. CARVER *picks up his son.*)

> That's why we were late. We spent the whole day digging tunnels. We're doing it for the dances tomorrow. Ha ha ha. We fooled you.

MOUNTAIN PEAK: That's an old one. A very old one. I haven't done that since I was a boy. Hoo hoo hoo hoo.

> (FOOL *is holding* ONE FOOT's *hand.* KETTLE *is mashing the berries, smiling.*)

FOOL: I thought you'd gone for good.

> (CARVER *takes* ONE FOOT *by the shoulder and pushes her towards the door.*)

CARVER: (*Harshly*) Go cook my supper. Now.

ONE FOOT: (*No longer laughing*) You can't give me orders. Can he? Must I cook?

MOUNTAIN PEAK: (*Bitterly*) I'm joining Great Chief Father Sun in bed.

CARVER: Go on.

KETTLE: Aren't you eating?

MOUNTAIN PEAK: I'll last clear through the winter. *My* store box is packed full. Look down upon the children made by you. Protect all those who came from you, Our Great Chief Father Sun.

ALL: Ha!

MOUNTAIN PEAK: Don't drink so deep there's no joy left tomorrow.

(*To* CARVER) I can't prevent you mucking up your life. Don't muck up my sleep.

(*To* KETTLE) Come cover me.

(*He goes out.*

KETTLE *takes her son from* CARVER *and goes out.*

CARVER *starts chipping again.*)

ONE FOOT: (*To* FOOL) Will you stop sewing buttons on blankets when we're married. I hope so.

(*To* CARVER) You never talk to people any more. That's why you're sad.

KETTLE: (*Off*) Bring the berries.

ONE FOOT: (*Still to* CARVER) Come talk to us while we cook the food. Make us squeal.

(*She embraces* FOOL.

Still to CARVER) Come on.

(*She goes out.*)

FOOL: The sky will be too dark to travel soon.

CARVER: My father almost ruined us once, paying blankets by the pile to have my mother cured. Her skin was rich with sores and boils. Every shaman had his turn and got his price. She died.

FOOL: But the son of Mamalelakwala dreamed of you. Go now.

CARVER: How do you know he's dying?

FOOL: You can't refuse me, boy. True shamans don't refuse.

CARVER: The wedding's off. Don't raise your voice. I'll pay back everything you've paid. Twice over. Sh. I'll spill your secrets.

FOOL: You're in it up to your neck.

CARVER: You lie. You cheat. You make us all your fools. Don't raise your voice! You've got a girl in every village up and down the coast. How else could you gather secrets? But that's no life for One Foot, married to a man who sneaks and creeps and crawls between two worlds. The mistake you made was opening my eyes. I loved you, boy. I'm not a shaman. I've lied too many times.

FOOL: You know the penalty for breaking secrecy.

22

CARVER: (*A sudden revelation*) Was Morning Climber drowned to make her free for you?

FOOL: Great Salmon River washed him over rapids. You saw the boat. They always claim they killed the boys who drown.

CARVER: A mist was clinging to my eyes. A grey toad leaps from stone to stone. I'm clinging to his foot.

FOOL: Did you break your vow?

CARVER: My people don't need you. We have our medicines. Kettle knows the recipes. We don't need tricks and secrecy. I want my place back.

FOOL: No.

CARVER: Give me my place. I'm not a shaman.

FOOL: Oh? Then why carve this?

CARVER: That pipe?

FOOL: This spirit catcher?

CARVER: It's a pipe!

(ONE FOOT *comes on*.)

ONE FOOT: Don't argue. Please. It's wrong.

CARVER: The wedding's off. I'll pay back everything he's paid.

(MOUNTAIN PEAK *comes on*.)

ONE FOOT: Oh no. Oh no. We've planned so many things. Oh father, make him change his mind. He says I'm not to marry Fool.

MOUNTAIN PEAK: On whose authority?

CARVER: My own.

(KETTLE *comes on*.)

MOUNTAIN PEAK: What reasons? Has he said? What are your reasons?

CARVER: You gave up your position. You're not the senior here.

FOOL: Nor you.

MOUNTAIN PEAK: Does Fool agree?

ONE FOOT: Oh Fool.

KETTLE: At midnight it will be the sacred season. Spirits are already in the house. They hear every word we say. We mustn't argue now. Carver would rather claw a tunnel through the earth than harm his sister. If he's made up his mind he has reasons.

ONE FOOT: Make him tell us what they are.

23

CARVER: He never stays at home. He's always wandering round.

ONE FOOT: Tell him, Kettle.

KETTLE: She's right, boy. So are you.

CARVER: He can't care for her properly. All he cares about is power.

MOUNTAIN PEAK: That's why I wish him well.

CARVER: It's wrong a man like him should be a chief. I have reasons none of you can understand.

MOUNTAIN PEAK: My words have reached the ocean floor. He feels the anger of his son grown up without a place, without his family's privileges. It's no use, boy. There's nothing for you here. You broke our line. You gave your father and son away.

(*Silence. Then* CARVER *goes out.*)

Thank Great Chief Father Sun I'm nearly dead. In this life only the worst survive.

(*He drinks.*)

Come cover me.

(*He goes out.*)

KETTLE: (*To* FOOL) Are you glad, boy? Then don't look glad. The spirits see it all.

(*She goes out.*

The rain starts up again.

FOOL *hands* ONE FOOT *a needle. She starts sewing a blanket.*)

FOOL: In the morning you can help me collect the blankets I'm owed. Eight thousand more or less. At noon I'll start my potlatch. I'll give them all away. I'll be seventh in the village. No arguments.

(*He puts a blanket round* ONE FOOT'*s shoulders.*)

Next year I'll claim my mother's father's place. That will be the biggest potlatch Fort Rupert's ever seen. We'll burn our house to ashes. Smash up our canoes. I'll be second in the village after that.

(CARVER *comes in. He puts his blanket round his shoulders.*

KETTLE *comes on, carrying food.*)

KETTLE: Oh not again. It's raining so hard now.

ONE FOOT: Don't be angry. Please. Don't go. You'll miss the dances.

24

CARVER: A son of the Mamalelakwala chief is dying.

KETTLE: We don't need what they pay you.

FOOL: Let him go.

KETTLE: Did they send a messenger?

(CARVER *nods*.)

Where is he? Does he want to eat? Or rest? Then how do you know he's dying?

CARVER: I'll be gone two days. He dreamed of me.

KETTLE: How will your son grow strong if he never has a father in the house?

CARVER: My son is strong if I am strong.

FOOL: He was chosen, Kettle. I'll take care of you.

KETTLE: But how do you *know* he's dying?

CARVER: I know because – because I feel I know. Because I am a shaman. I *am* a shaman. I know. I simply know.

(*He goes out quickly. The rain is very hard.*)

THREE

Winter 1875.

WHALE, *Chief of the Bela Coola, in ceremonial dress, holds the speaker's staff without which no one may address the people. He holds a large, elaborately carved copper ornament in his arms. He bangs the staff four times on the ground. It rattles as he bangs it.*

WHALE: I, Chief Whale of the Bela Coola, greet the sun on this third day of our winter dances. Chief Fool of the Kwakiutl will buy a copper from me today. The name of my great copper is No Blankets in the House. Eight winter dances ago I bought it for my people. The price was seven thousand blankets. Bela Coola! Enough. That is all.

WHALE'S FOLLOWERS: Ah! Ah! Ah! Ah! (*Etc.*)

(FOOL *takes the staff.*)

FOOL: O Great Chief Whale of the Bela Coola. We are Kwakiutl! We have never been vanquished by any tribe. Not in wars of blood or wars of property. In olden times you Bela Coola fought against our fathers and stained the rocks blood red. Now we fight with blankets and we smile at one another. Oh how good is this new smiling time. I have twelve thousand blankets for No Blankets in the House. Kwakiutl! Enough.

25

That is all.

(*Whenever* FOOL *makes an offer for the copper, one of his men goes across to* WHALE *to fetch the copper and is surprised when* WHALE *draws back and demands an even higher price.*)

FOOL'S FOLLOWERS: Ah! Ah! Ah! Ah! (*Etc.*)

(WHALE *confers with one of the Bela Coola men. He takes the staff.*)

WHALE: But wait. We know you are a great man, Fool. We know that you Kwakiutl are rich and powerful men. We know you Kwakiutl believe: he is the strongest man who gives the most away. We know you do not wish to buy this copper for less than the most you can afford. Is this right what I am saying?

WHALE'S FOLLOWERS: Yes, yes, yes, it is right.

WHALE: Now, Fool. I knew that when I said the price was seven thousand blankets you would offer far more than I asked. But so that you may prove to all your followers how great a man you are, I will ask for far more than you gave. You offered me twelve thousand blankets. So, I am asking twenty thousand blankets for No Blankets in the House.

WHALE'S FOLLOWERS: Ah! Ah! Ah! Ah! (*Etc.*)

(FOOL *confers with one of his men. He takes the staff.*)

FOOL: I say, we can give you what you ask and more. We have never been defeated by any tribe. Our payments have always been the greatest ever made. If you ask twenty thousand blankets we will give you twenty-five.

FOOL'S FOLLOWERS: Ah! Ah! Ah! Ah! (*Etc.*)

(WHALE *takes the staff.*)

WHALE: Friends, no wonder Kwakiutl hunters can't trap bears and have no skill in stalking deer. They have no ears.

(*Laughter.*)

I have never mentioned twenty thousand. I said the price of this great copper is thirty thousand blankets.

WHALE'S FOLLOWERS: Ah! Ah! Ah! Ah!

(FOOL *takes the staff.*)

FOOL: Friends, it is known that when you eat you splash your clothes with half-chewed fish. Now we see why. Your thoughts have no control over your tongues.

(*The people laugh and clap.* FOOL *confers with one of his men.*)

But friends, even if by mistake you ask for thirty thousand

26

blankets, we will give you thirty-five.

ALL: Ai! Ai! Ai! Ai! (*Etc.*)

(*Applause. A woman leaps up, embraces* FOOL *and dances ecstatically. She is pulled down by the others.*
WHALE *takes the staff.*)

WHALE: Friends, you Kwakiutl have heard us well and we have spoken what is in our minds. But – we are told the great chiefs never buy for less than the most they can afford. We know the Kwakiutl are the great chiefs of the world. See!
(*He holds a piece of coal in one hand.*)
To search if anywhere there may be greater men than these, I send him round the world –
(*He whirls his hand round his head to indicate the boundaries of their world and then he throws the coal into the air. It vanishes. He remains still and silent until it completes its circuit of the world and returns. He plucks it from the air and holds it to his ear.*)
And he says no. There are no greater men in all the world than the Kwakiutl. So, we say – Fool! Great Chief of the Kwakiutl. This is the greatest, most expensive, famous, powerful copper there has ever been. The price of No Blankets in the House is fifty thousand blankets.
(*Silence.*)

PEOPLE: The house is burning! The fire has caught the walls! The house is burning!

FOOL: Let the walls burn! Let the roof burn! Let the beams crash down on the rocks! Let our great ancestral statues be devoured by the flames! Let it eat my boats sailing on my rivers! Let it swallow my trees growing in my forests! Let every standing timber crack and fall!
(*The fire spreads quickly.* FOOL *stands triumphant, holding the staff between his hands above his head. He breaks it and throws it down. He tears off his decorations and throws them down. He is naked to the waist.*)
We pay you sixty thousand blankets!
(*Silence. The sound of fire.*
Then:)

ALL: Ha! Ha! Ha! Ha!

(*Growing to a crescendo. One of* FOOL's *men fetches the copper from* WHALE.)

FOOL: Kwakiutl!

ALL: Kwakiutl!

FOOL: Kwakiutl!

ALL: Kwakiutl!

(WHALE *retires defeated. Two men present* FOOL *with the copper which he holds high. Stamping, whistling, hooting, dancing.* FOOL *takes the copper off. The others follow.*)

FOUR

Spring 1876.
Night. The room is small and lit by a fire in the next room. CARVER *sits, eating from a bowl.* KETTLE *sits some distance apart, sewing.*

CARVER: I skimmed the surface of the stream as light as any water walking fly. The villages slid by. When I reached the sea I trapped a halibut in my hands and ate my first meal in two days.
(*He eats.*)

KETTLE: A plank in the seaside wall fell out. Sand blew in. I asked my brother Fool to mend it. Bear Face patched it up before he had the chance. They'd do anything for you and yours.

CARVER: Dancer's face looks flushed. Did he run about before he went to sleep?

KETTLE: You didn't wake him? He's full of energy that boy. I took them out to play at Candle Rock. Your daughter cut her leg. I bound it up with squid skin. It wasn't deep.

CARVER: By Tower Rock a clot of birds came winging just above the sea, came flying from behind and over me as if I wasn't there. A streaming, pink streaked cloud. And I was up there, with them, out across the sea. This island's deep in mystery. Even when we think we understand, he's only put his nose out of the stream. This is for you.
(*He gives her a gold necklace.*)
I cured the great chief's son.
(*He puts it round her neck.*)

28

It's worth two thousand blankets.

KETTLE: Is there a spirit in it?

CARVER: Ha ha ha.

KETTLE: It throws out light like fire. Look. It smiles at me. Two
thousand blankets. It'll keep me very warm.

(CARVER *spreads a mat on the floor.* KETTLE *lays a mat away
from him.*)

I'll wear it round my neck until Bird marries. She'll give it to
her daughter. Our family will always know the day they
called you Quesalid.

(*She lies down.* CARVER *drags his mat over to her and lies beside
her. She sits up.*)

CARVER: Lie, treasure. Make me warm.

(*She stands.*)

KETTLE: The back door isn't barred.

(*She goes off, comes back in.*)

Weaver's child vanished three days ago. Just went into the
air. That's the second child to vanish in five days. Where do
they go? I don't let Bird or Dancer out of my sight. They said
they'll come to ask you for your help.

(*She drags her mat away from* CARVER.)

Don't be angry with me. I may not sleep with you.

(*She lies down. He gets up and sits beside her.*)

CARVER: You always punish me when I come home. My love, my
sweet. These strangers send for me to care for them. It's a
duty power gives a man. I have to cure my people when they
call.

KETTLE: The Koskimo were never our people.

CARVER: Isn't this worth a husband for eight days? No other Fort
Rupert wife has anything so rare and valuable.

KETTLE: You men, you men. You understand the secrets, all the
mysteries. Why don't you understand your wives? I don't
want presents.

(*She throws the necklace aside.*)

CARVER: That's two thousand blankets.

KETTLE: I want *you*.

(*He fetches the necklace and puts it round his neck. He drags his
mat over to hers.*)

CARVER: Tomorrow we'll go to Singing Rock. It's time to teach the children how to swim.

KETTLE: I wish you'd go out fishing with your friends. Fish you catch yourself are twice as tasty.

CARVER: Fish grateful patients put in your hand taste pretty good as well.

(*He lies down.*)

Look. It's glittering. Treasure. I hate to see you cry. Let me lick them. There. Press up close.

(*She drags her mat away.*)

KETTLE: I may not sleep with you.

CARVER: (*In a rage*) Get out! Get out! No, come here. Come to me.

(*He goes to her. She turns away.*)

What are you shaking for?

KETTLE: I may not sleep with you. Don't make me.

CARVER: Lie down.

(*She lies down.*)

I'm not angry any more. Sleep.

(*He lies down.*)

I can wait until tomorrow.

KETTLE: I may not sleep with you for one full year.

CARVER: Are you ill? What's happened? Answer me.

KETTLE: If I tell it's bad luck for us both. Especially you.

CARVER: I'm not sleeping in the same house as a whore.

(*He goes out, comes back in.*)

KETTLE: I never touched another man.

CARVER: (*Raging*) Great Quesalid has grown too old for you. You've tasted younger flesh. You like its sharp tang more.

KETTLE: I want you. I long for you. My body aches to press itself against you, cup itself inside you, feel your strong hands pressing on my skin.

CARVER: (*Broken*) Don't cry, my love. Don't cry.

KETTLE: I may not do it. Please. Be patient with me. Wait.

CARVER: (*Raging, again*) A year? Till I grow bored and let you have your way? When I come back I want you out. Your children. Clothes. Your basket tools. Take every thing that stinks of you and go. Except my son.

(*He goes out. He rushes back and embraces her.*)
Come hold me. Like this. Sitting. See? That's right. We're
not lying now. Hold me. There. Strong hands on your skin.
Now. What happened?

KETTLE: He told me not to say.

CARVER: Whatever spell or curse or charm it is I'll break it with
my blood. Don't cry! Tell me.

KETTLE: The day you went away, he stood on the quay in front of
Weaver's house. He stared at me. I stared at him. I can't say
why. Sharp features, tall and very pale as if he'd hidden in
dark corners all his life and what he saw there gave him his
mocking grin. I'd never seen a face like that before. So pale.
That night I barred the door and lay down on the mat. The
door blew open wide and there he stood. He took off all his
clothes. He lay down by my side. I tried to move away. I
couldn't. I tried to feel him there, to push him out. I
couldn't. He didn't touch me – ever. But I felt strong – so
strong and warm and kind. He told me he would come to lie
beside me four nights in a row. He told me he would leave a
bundle with me which would bring us great good fortune,
both of us. But only if I did not lie with you for one full year
and if I did not tell you that he came. He lay with me four
nights, last night the last. He never touched me once. Not
once. I swear. He said: tell your husband and you'll suffer
great misfortune. Last night he left the bundle and going
said he'd never come again.

CARVER: Where is the bundle?

KETTLE: Where?

CARVER: Let me see it.

KETTLE: We may not open it.

CARVER: Let me see.
(*She goes to fetch it.*)

KETTLE: It's gone. I wrapped it in this cloth. It's gone.

CARVER: I hear this tale in every village up and down the coast.
Who said to tell me this?

KETTLE: It's gone. He told me not to tell.

CARVER: Who shared your mat while I was gone?

KETTLE: No one touched my body from the day you left till now.

CARVER: He took off all his clothes and lay down on your mat.

KETTLE: I didn't feel his toe against my side.

CARVER: I've heard this story up and down the coast. I tell the husbands: don't believe a word, a word. Don't let them go until you want them out. Under all your softnesses, your shows of love, you women hate us men. You wish you never had to cook our food or feel our flesh. You tell those lies to wear us down till, brokenhearted, in despair, we send you home. Who said to tell me this? I'll break her scheming neck.

KETTLE: It's true. He came. He told me not to tell.

CARVER: When face to face with truth most wives recant, embrace their husbands, take them to their beds. But you – you'd still insist the truth shines from your face if I slice fingers off your hand, your hand from off your wrist and feed them to the goats. I travelled four days, cradling this room, that mat, your breast in my mind's eye. Now all I want is sleep. Just tell me – Kettle, answer me – remember who I am and what I know – one last time, tell me: is your story true?

KETTLE: In the five years we've been married we haven't quarrelled once. I promise not to tell. I break my word. And now –

CARVER: You don't want husbands. You want children. Now you've got them any lie, any tale that swims into your head and off back home. You will not take my son.

KETTLE: The children.

CARVER: Stay where you are!

KETTLE: I broke my word. Don't let him hurt the children. (*She runs out.*)

CARVER: Women. Clouds. The slightest breeze sends them soaring, streaming up and up until they smash against the skies and pour themselves as hail upon the earth. What should be sweet and welcome as spring rain tears every fragile living thing to shreds.

(KETTLE *comes in.*)

KETTLE: Dancer's in a fever.

CARVER: He's flushed. That's all. You let him run too late.

KETTLE: He's moaning in his sleep. His mat is damp with sweat. We're being punished.

32

CARVER: No.

(He hesitates, then goes out.

She pours water into a bowl.)

KETTLE: I'm not worried. You can cure him. You're stronger than the stranger. Any spell or curse or charm.

(KETTLE stirs roots and herbs into the water. CARVER comes in.)

CARVER: His face is grey. He's shivering.

KETTLE: Suck the sickness from him. Go on. Go on!

CARVER: Oh, Kettle.

KETTLE: Is this what strangers pay you for? To watch you shake, tears welling in your eye? I'll heat the water. Take his shirt off him.

(He takes the gold necklace off.)

CARVER: The world is full of lies. I thought that I could lead them, keep them like an eagle on a string. They grow so fast and fly so hard they drag us tumbling after. I'm not a shaman. I can't cure his sickness.

KETTLE: Every week you go off curing strangers.

CARVER: He's my son!

KETTLE: They send for you from up and down the coast.

CARVER: I'm not a shaman.

(He takes a feather from under his upper lip.)

See this feather? I keep it underneath my lip. I pretend to find the sickness. I suck and suck. I bite my cheek to make blood flow. It's blood from my cheeks that flows.

I wash the feather in the blood inside my mouth. I suck four times. I spit the feather out. I show it saying: I hold the sickness in my hand. The feather seems to wriggle in my palm. I plunge it deep in water. I tell him: you're free of sickness. I throw this feather far into the sea. That's how it's done. I have no power. I'm lost in thick night's tangle. No way out before me, no way out behind. My wife has lied. My son is sick –

KETTLE: Then do that to him.

CARVER: I put it in my mouth. It's not a worm.

KETTLE: Suck the feather from his side. I'll heat the water.

(She goes off.)

CARVER: *(Calls)* I hide the feather underneath my lip. I'm not a

33

shaman. Kettle! I can't cure sickness.

KETTLE: (*Off*) The fire's high. Come on.

(*As* CARVER *attempts to put himself under the control of the wolf spirit that guides him when he cures, his face contorts in a snarl, his body is tense and expectant. It has no effect. He tries again, growling and pawing. He utters the cry of the raven that* BLOOD LIP *made before.*)

CARVER: Kama ka kei. Kama ka kei.

(*The spirit will not come. He gives up. And then his body seems to stiffen of its own accord. He howls like the woman shaman in Scene One, but it is broken off. He seems to be resisting his possession, clawing his way out. Or is it the wolf spirit contorting his hands into claws? He follows* KETTLE *out.*)

(*In falsetto, off*) Oh friends, where have I been and who has carried me home?

(*We hear him retching up the sickness he has sucked from his son's body. All the sounds are echoes of* BLOOD LIP's *curing in Scene 1.*)

(*Off*) I hold the sickness in my hand. Aiiii!

(*He comes on. He finds he has something stuck to his hand and throws it on the ground. He sits.* KETTLE *comes on.*)

KETTLE: The colour's flowing back into his cheeks. He didn't even wake. He's breathing gently now.

(*She kisses him.*)

Your face is like a rock with weariness. Look at me, boy.

(*He does. She lies down on her mat.*)

Sleep now.

(CARVER *drags his mat to hers and lies down.* KETTLE *gets up, drags her mat away and lies on it.* CARVER *stands, takes off his belt, holds it in his hand.*)

CARVER: When you touch my cheek your fingers curl back to your hand. Get up. Lie on my mat. Move.

KETTLE: Dancer's fever was a sign.

CARVER: I empty my body of its lies. You force my vomit down my throat again. Lie on my mat. Move, woman. Move.

KETTLE: I can't.

(*He hits her with his belt.*)

I mustn't. I swear. He said. It's true.

(*His rage passes. She weeps.*)

34

CARVER: In the north among the Bela Coola lives the shaman Life
    Owner. I believe that he is the one true shaman in the world.
    And for these reasons. His patients never pay him for their
    cure. No one has ever seen Life Owner smile. Other shamans
    show their patients nothing. You're cured, they say. That's
    all. At least from me they get a wriggling worm.
    (*He lies on his mat.*)
BETSY HUNT: I tell you what my father said and also what I
    heard. I will not swear that what I say is true. Our people
    need a Quesalid again. We have a need. We are not whole.
    We Kwakiutl say: grandparent lives in grandchild. As
    fisherman perhaps or storyteller and so on. He held me in his
    arms when I was small and soft as clay. Some part of him
    lives on in me. I have no power, no. But Quesalid was
    famous for his storytelling too. Perhaps that part of me I
    have from him. So let it speak to you.

FIVE

Winter 1886.
The DANCERS *enter. Some are idiot dancers (the Kwakiutl) who wear*
long pointy noses and some are grizzly bear dancers (the Bela Coola)
who wear ears and furs. The idiot dancers' clothes have decorations
painted only in black, the bear dancers' in black and red.

First performance:
DANCERS: (*Sing*)
    My love streams through my body like a pain.
    My love streams through my body like a pain.
    Fire burns and sickness grows,
    House beams stand as black as crows,
    From my mouth my red blood flows.
    My love streams through my body like a pain.

    My true love rows away across the bay.
    Will he never turn his boat again this way?
    Sickness grows and fire burns,
    This is what the lover learns:

Joy and pain must take their turns.
Pain rows through my body out across the bay.

BETSY HUNT: My cousin called me on the telephone. He said:
We're going to hold a potlatch. Will you come? I said: there
hasn't been a potlatch held in thirty years. No one knows
their places now. But he said: yes, he'd read those books my
father helped write down. He'd spent a year and worked it
out again. I told him: boy, if you're going to do this potlatch,
do it well. Wait till winter comes. Do the dances. They used
to do all kinds of dances. Spectacles and plays. If anyone felt
bad against another man he'd get his own back in a dance.
They'd laugh at all the things that made them sad: what
brother did to brother, man to wife. And when the white
men came, each year the dances would bind up our peoples'
wounds. My father told me all about those times. We're
Christians now. But those times are bright – bright in my
eye.

(FOOL *holds the speaker's staff. He bangs it four times on the
ground. It rattles as he bangs it.*)

FOOL: Friends –

BEARS: Go away. Don't speak to us. Get off.

IDIOTS: He holds the staff! You can't interrupt a man who holds
the staff.

BEARS: Let Whale speak to us. Not him. Let Whale speak. Go
away!

FOOL: Friends, we welcome to our home –

BEARS: Waaaaa! Go home yourself!

FOOL: We welcome –

A BEAR: We'd welcome the sight of your arse.

(*Laughter. An idiot dancer clobbers a bear dancer.* FOOL *bangs
the staff. The fighting spreads.*)

AN IDIOT: No fighting while the chief is speaking! No fighting
while the great chief holds the staff!

Second performance:

FOOL *puts a glove puppet of a man dressed in a bear dancer's costume
on his hand. Immediately the commotion dies away.* FOOL *speaks
through the glove puppet.*

36

FOOL: We welcome our friends the Bela Coola and their Chief
Whale to the second day of our winter dances.

Third performance:
*A real grizzly bear comes on. He claws and snarls and snaps. The
people are terrified and try to run away.* BETSY HUNT,
*fascinated and in some way awakened by the bear, puts on a
pointy nose and joins the* DANCERS.

FOOL: Tame him. He must be tamed. Don't scream. Don't cry.
Don't run away. Teach him to dance. Teach him to dance.
(*He bangs his staff on the ground. A chorus is taken up:*)

DANCERS: Teach him to dance. Teach him to dance.
(*One man begins singing the second song. Others join in. At first
the bear ignores them. They start to dance. By the end they are all
dancing with the bear.*)

DANCERS: (*Sing*)
Baby, baby, all the people call me baby.
Who sleeps through the day and screams all night?
Baby, baby.
Who pisses in the food and pukes on the bed?
Baby, baby.
Who eats and eats and never works?
Baby, baby.
Who puts his finger up the little girl's cunt?
Baby, baby, all the people call me baby.
(*The bear lies down and* FOOL *puts his foot on its back. The
dancers applaud, whistle and stamp.* FOOL *bangs his staff four
times on the ground.*)

FOOL: I am the Great Chief Fool. My name is famous among all
tribes for I have given blankets to them all. Now I am chief
of the winter ceremonial at this time of year when all the
stones turn over.
(*The bear scampers out.*)

IDIOTS: Your words are true! Your words are good, Chief. Go on!
Teach your children how to speak!

FOOL: Now let me speak to you. Yesterday I gave blankets to you
all, Kwakiutl, Bela Coola, each according to your place.
Today is the potlatch of Chief Whale.

(WHALE *takes the staff and bangs it four times on the ground*.)

WHALE: Friends, you all know my name. You knew my father. He was a thoughtless, wasteful man. He killed his slaves or threw them in the sea. He gave away canoes. He burnt his house. He cut deer skins to shreds. He threw thousands of sea otter skins away. Do as my father did. Take the blankets the Kwakiutl give you and tear them into shreds. The war we are waging now is sweet and strong. When I perform my potlatch we'll give them five times more than they gave us yesterday. Bela Coola! Enough. That is all.

BEARS: Ah! Ah! Ah! Ah! (*Etc.*)

Fourth performance:

The light becomes dim. In the distance, the sound of
CANNIBAL DANCERS.

CANNIBAL DANCERS: Hap! Hap! Hap! Hap!

(*The* CANNIBAL DANCERS *burst in. They wear the enormous masks of the Cannibal Birds, complete with snapping jaws to crush their victims' skulls. They dance jerkily, shaking about, blood and saliva running from their mouths. They attack whoever is near them, snapping at them, trying to bite their arms and necks. They take limbs of a human body from a box. They tear off chunks with their teeth and swallow them. Their mouths and fingers run with blood. Their dance becomes more frenzied. They grunt and snort and stamp. The women squeal, first in delight, then in horror and fear. The dance becomes more menacing. Now the dancers lunge at the women snapping and snarling.*

The two women run to the side. A cannibal chases them. They cry out and laugh, almost hysterical. Another cannibal claws at BETSY HUNT *and runs up against her. The terror of the women is quite spontaneous and real but for* BETSY HUNT *it rises until she cannot contain it. The dancers are wild and after blood. A cannibal grabs* BETSY HUNT, *one hand on her breast, the other on her back. She screams.*

KETTLE *runs to one side, pours water into a bowl, adds bits of root and brings it to* BETSY HUNT. CARVER *holds* BETSY HUNT *by the back of her head and presses on her temples.*

38

She faints. CARVER *eases her to the ground.*)

FOOL: Friends, there is no cause to fear. Our mighty shaman
　　Quesalid will suck the sickness out.

WHALE: No!

　　(LIFE OWNER *wears a red band round his head. He swings his
　　rattle.*)

LIFE OWNER: You say that you are hungry?

　　(*He puts his rattle to his ear.*)

　　I am hungry too.

　　(*He places the rattle on the palm of his left hand. He lets it go.
　　His hand quivers. The rattle hovers underneath his palm.*)

　　I am Life Owner, shaman of the Bela Coola.

　　(*He grabs the rattle and shakes it.*)

　　He says that he is hungry. Sickness entered this woman as
　　she passed in front of me. I am the shaman that will draw it
　　out of her.

　　(*He shakes his rattle.* FOOL *takes the speaker's staff.*)

FOOL: O Bela Coola, I am the chief of this winter ceremonial.
　　This woman is of my people. We Kwakiutl possess the
　　greatest shaman in the world. Enough. That is all.

　　(WHALE *takes the staff.*)

WHALE: O Kwakiutl in the last five summers my people have
　　suffered many new diseases. Everyone Life Owner treated is
　　feasting with us now. Let the Bela Coola save this day. Let
　　Life Owner save this woman. Enough. That is all.

　　(FOOL *tries to take the staff.* WHALE *will not let it go. They tug
　　at it. Then they throw it down and stand glaring at each other.
　　Silence. The sound of birds is heard.*)

A MAN: Let them compete!

DANCERS: Let them compete. Yes. Let them compete. Let them
　　see who cures her first. True words. Let them compete.

　　(DANCER *takes up the staff.*)

DANCER: I say: let my father pit his strength against this shaman.
　　We do not fight in battles now. But let these shamans fight
　　for us. Let these shamans fight to save this woman and their
　　names.

PEOPLE: Let them compete. Let them compete. (*Etc.*)

　　(FOOL *takes the staff.*)

FOOL: You have spoken. They shall compete. To the winner goes the title: shaman of the world.

ALL: Ah! Ah! Ah! Ah! (*Etc.*)

(BETSY HUNT *is carried out.* CARVER *and* FOOL *remain.*)

FOOL: Go on. They're waiting for you.

CARVER: I can't compete with him.

FOOL: Go on!

CARVER: You know Life Owner is the one true shaman in the world. Why didn't you warn me, boy?

FOOL: Boy, I can't plan everything. But go. They're waiting.

CARVER: No. He'll make her well. These dances make you our greatest chief. Now stop. Don't lose it all.

PEOPLE: (*Off*) Quesalid! Quesalid! Where is he? Quesalid!

FOOL: Go!

(CARVER *pulls* FOOL *to one side.*)

CARVER: If it was any other curing man I would. And win. But I can't face Life Owner armed with tricks.

FOOL: And him? He never smiles. That's his trick.

CARVER: Is that all you understand? He's real.

FOOL: How, real? You tell me what is real.

CARVER: Life Owner's strength. His power. He never takes reward.

FOOL: And me? What's my reward? I'm speaking for our people.

PEOPLE: (*Off*) Quesalid! Quesalid!

FOOL: Make that woman well, the Bela Coola will be (*Spits*) dead fish.

CARVER: You push me deeper, deeper in the muck.

FOOL: You call this muck? You fail, I lose my life. Or everything that makes it worth the living. Would I take that risk? I know your strength.

PEOPLE: (*Off*) Quesalid!

CARVER: (*In anguish*) Fool –

FOOL: When we were young the chiefs and shamans were like the mountains on the moon. No man on earth could ever climb so high. Now (*gestures*) – you've got to recognize the thing you are. You've never treated patients with anything but 'tricks'.

CARVER: No.

FOOL: And yet you've never failed. How can that be? How can a
trick be turned into a truth? Boy? Can a boat row itself across
the strait? No. Only when a man heaves on the oars. Call a
boat a trick for crossing water. Call a spear a trick for
catching a fish. The power *is* in you. In *you*. Here. Here. And
here. And here.
(*He embraces* CARVER.)
You've never failed before. They're waiting. Go. And win
for us again.
(CARVER *goes off*.
FOOL *cuts his arm with a knife*.)
Oh Great Chief Father Sun, look after me. Let this be noon
not night. Just this one last time.
(*Whistling and cries of*: '*Quesalid!*' *off, at* CARVER'*s arrival.
The cries die away.
FOOL stands alone a long moment, exhausted, bleeding. Then he
binds his arm and roars out:*)
Friends!
(*He waits. The* DANCERS *enter*.)
It is not wise to watch the shamans work. Ha ha. While they
fight to save that woman's life, listen to me. I remember all
the oldest tales. Far off echoes of a stream. Be silent. Listen.
This is how when light came to the world, men were born
and how the world began.

Fifth performance:
I am Great Chief Father Sun. This is the sky, my home. In
days gone by I lived here in tranquillity and peace. But men
on earth have grown indifferent to my rule. All day they
sing. Their games and laughter stir up such a din I hardly
close my eyes and I'm awake. Is all this noise in praise of me?
They hardly know I'm here. So I let the rain fall from the
sky. And it will rain till all the rivers flood their banks, the
villages drown and only mountain peaks protrude. Noses on
the great face of the deep. No more squealing men. Now I
can sleep in peace.
(*He indicates a woman – who will play the* MOTHER – *and two
men –* FATHER *and* SON.)

41

MOTHER: Son, hold tightly to the raft. We've been floating many
  years. There's no food left to eat. If the waters don't drain
  soon we'll die. Lay your head in my lap. I'll comfort you.

FATHER: Wife, don't spoil the boy. We're not worth saving. I'm a
  fisherman. I know how cursed are men. Pray to Great Chief
  Father Sun to turn us into rocks. Then we can tumble from
  this raft and live below the sea. Our great curse, wife, is what
  you offer to our son. The softness of our skin.

GREAT CHIEF FATHER SUN: You are the last three living in the
  world. Praise me.

SON: Look. Birds are gathering in the sky.

MOTHER: Great clouds of eagles gathering in the sky.

FATHER: They're shedding feathers down on to the sea.

SON: The mountain's rising. The sea is sinking. We're saved.
  We're saved.

GREAT CHIEF FATHER SUN: But you will live on rocky ground for
  all your lives. If you dance too joyfully the rocks will cut your
  feet. Then you'll remember what you owe to me. What is
  your name, boy?

SON: My name is –

GREAT CHIEF FATHER SUN: (*Interrupts, whispering*) Fool.
  (SON, *surprised, looks to the others for confirmation.* FOOL *prods
  him.*)
  Fool!

SON: My name is Fool.

GREAT CHIEF FATHER SUN: Then listen, Fool. I have chosen you
  of all your tribe to rescue from the flood. As a sign that I have
  cared for you, the children that you bear will always be the
  chief men of your tribe. The Kwakiutl will stay powerful as
  long as they are ruled by Great Chief Fool. In the winter
  months they'll dance as I instruct them to and sing great
  praise of me.

Sixth performance:
*Two men wearing white masks and dressed to represent policemen
  burst in.*

POLICEMAN 1: Whose house is this?

POLICEMAN 2: Who's celebrating here?

POLICEMAN 1: Will everyone here put up his hand? Good. All here.

POLICEMAN 2: Now, everyone not here put up his hand. Good. Nobody isn't here.

POLICEMAN 1: Take down their names.

POLICEMAN 2: Bar the doors. Take down their names.

(*The* POLICEMEN *go round taking down people's names.*)

FOOL (AS JUDGE): Who's first to be tried, convicted and jailed?

POLICEMAN 1: There's someone missing here. This seat's unoccupied.

FOOL (AS JUDGE): Well done. The seat is here but empty so the occupant must be somewhere else. Well done.

POLICEMAN 2: I've found the woman, sir. She says she can't come now. She's feeding her child.

FOOL (AS JUDGE): Feeding her child? Rubbish. These people leave their children in the rain to starve. I'll fetch her myself.

(*The* JUDGE *goes off.*)

POLICEMAN 2: I saw a pile of blankets by her door.

POLICEMAN 1: How many?

POLICEMAN 2: Seventy.

POLICEMAN 1: Better make a note of that.

POLICEMAN 2: She-has-seventy-button-blankets. There.

(*The* JUDGE *comes on pulling a long rope. At the end is* ONE FOOT.)

FOOL (AS JUDGE): Now. What's this? Seventy blankets? Do you own seventy blankets?

(ONE FOOT *nods.*)

That's – ah – thirty-five dollars. You've committed a very serious crime indeed.

POLICEMAN 1: Your honour, she wasn't present but refused to raise her hand to indicate that fact.

FOOL (AS JUDGE): Excellent. Two crimes in one. Guilty or not guilty?

POLICEMAN 2: (*In falsetto*) Guilty.

FOOL (AS JUDGE): Fined seventy blankets. Lock her up. Next.

ONE FOOT: Your honour, you've taken all my blankets. Must you lock me up as well?

FOOL (AS JUDGE): Of course. If you're set free, you'll go straight home and commit your crime again. Lock her up in that box there.

(POLICEMAN 1 *and* 2 *put* ONE FOOT *into the box.*)

That'll keep her in one place. Now. To make sure she never commits her crime again –

(*He thrusts a spear through the box. The other* DANCERS *cry out in horror. The* JUDGE *pulls the spear out and opens the box. It is empty. The* DANCERS *applaud and cheer. He closes the door. He opens it and* BETSY HUNT *steps out. She has been cured. She smiles, waves goodbye to her memories and leaves the main acting area. The* JUDGE *closes the box, opens it and* CARVER, *the victorious shaman, steps out. He looks bewildered.*)

FOOL: Quesalid has sucked out the sickness!

(CARVER *throws out his arms and the* DANCERS *cheer his victory.*)

DANCERS: Aaaaaaaaaah!

(KETTLE *throws her arms round* CARVER's *neck and embraces him.* FOOL *places a red band round* CARVER's *head.*)

FOOL: Quesalid has defeated the Bela Coola!

DANCERS: Aaaaaaaaaah!

FOOL: Quesalid is the greatest shaman in the world!

(*Great clapping, singing, stamping, dancing. They all go out.*
CARVER *is left alone.*
Whistling off, briefly.
KETTLE *brings* CARVER *a bowl of food.*)

KETTLE: I knew you couldn't lose, boy.

CARVER: Take care of Dancer.

KETTLE: And Bird?

CARVER: And Bird. And Bird. And you.

KETTLE: Eat, boy.

CARVER: Kettle, girl – our life is changed.

KETTLE: Won't you need to eat now? I'll try to be a good wife.
Will it be hard?

(CARVER *nods.*)

Oh, boy.

(*She goes to embrace him. He turns away, looks at his hands.*
KETTLE *takes the bowl out.*

Bird-song.
CARVER *looks up.* FOOL *comes in.*)
FOOL: I don't see any muck.
(*He laughs.* CARVER *laughs.*)
Whale's put off his potlatch. It'll take a year to collect the blankets to defeat us now. His men are drawing family trees to trace their Kwakiutl ancestry. Ha!
CARVER: These hands.
FOOL: Now, boy. You've got one action left.
CARVER: I must talk to Life Owner.
FOOL: No!
CARVER: I must make my peace with him or he'll send his power after me.
FOOL: Carver!
CARVER: Listen to me now, boy. I have power. Yes. But he must teach me how to master it. These hands. Whose are they? Fool? Who owns these hands? I have to learn.
(FOOL *grabs* CARVER's *hands.*)
FOOL: For seven years I was a dreamer. Endless rowing up and down the coast. The deadly cold of night. I lived my life in darkness, boy. The moon my only friend. I thought then: shamans have the sharpest power, yes. But I will have such strength that I can live in Father Sun's bright day.
CARVER: I have to learn!
FOOL: Yes! But not from him. You've beaten him. What can he teach you now? You must leave the island.
CARVER: Leave?
FOOL: Take Kettle, Dancer, Bird. Cross the strait. I'll send you patients.
CARVER: I'm weak.
FOOL: If they have to travel far they'll pay you well. It hasn't sunk in, boy. He's finished. You're the greatest shaman now.
(*Silence.*)
CARVER: If I have power to heal, Fool, I have power to harm. Let him come.
(*Singing off.*
LIFE OWNER *and* SKY *come in.* LIFE OWNER *is not wearing his red band.*)

All my life I've waited for you. If you will teach me I will
learn.

LIFE OWNER: It won't be bad what we say to one another, friend.

(CARVER *gestures at* FOOL.

FOOL, *with great reluctance, goes out.*)

My daughter, Sky.

(CARVER *gestures them to sit. He pours water from a bowl into
cups and offers one to* LIFE OWNER, *who drinks.*)

I have come to plead with you to save my life. You have
made me a toy to my people. A doll – flung aside. I will die of
shame. What stuck to the palm of your hand? Was it the
sickness?

(*He puts his rattle to his palm. He lets it go. It hangs there. He
pushes it. It swings. He opens his fingers. It falls. He picks it up
and points to its stem.*)

A nail. (*He smiles.*) Now tell me what you do.

CARVER: But the people never pay you.

(*Bird-song.*)

LIFE OWNER: Oh no. Oh no no no. Ha ha ha ha. People never
pay me. That would spoil it all. Whale pays me. Ha ha ha ha.
Whale's father thought it out. He used to pay me too. Ha ha.
But not the people, no. For every man I cure, Whale pays me
thirty dollars. I'll pay you for your secret. Then I can do it
too. How much?

(CARVER *takes the red band from his head. His voice breaks as
he speaks.*)

CARVER: It will soon be daylight. We must not be seen.

SKY: How can he live? Pity him. How can my father live?

(CARVER *wets the red band in the bowl and throws it into*
LIFE OWNER'*s face.*)

CARVER: Life Owner, shaman of the Bela Coola, I will show you
which of our things are true.

(*As he speaks the* DANCERS *enter without masks.* CARVER
speaks to them.)

This box. People appear and disappear. The spirits guide
them? No. The back is false and on a hinge. They slip in or
creep away along this passage here.

46

(He reveals the trap door under the box.)

DANCERS: Any child knows that. Why is he telling us? We know
that.

CARVER: This isn't human flesh.

DANCERS: We know that. Does he think we're fools? Of course
we know it wasn't human flesh.

CARVER: It's fish tied to deer's bones.

(He bites it.)

DANCERS: We know.

CARVER: *(His desperation growing)* They aren't real cannibals.
They fooled you.

DANCERS: No they didn't. We knew that. We've seen all that
before. We know. We know.

CARVER: It's trickery. My whole life's trickery. Everything you
see is trickery! And now you'll see the greatest trick of all.
(Silence. He takes a feather from underneath his lip.)

Seventh performance:

FOOL *takes out a gun. The* DANCERS *see it.* CARVER *sees it.* KETTLE
cries out.

FOOL *shoots* CARVER. CARVER *staggers but does not fall.* FOOL
rushes up to CARVER *and catches him in his arms.* DANCER
rushes up.

KETTLE: Carver!

*(*CARVER *has not been hurt.* DANCER *and* FOOL *back away,
amazed.)*

CARVER: And then I realized, yes! I am the greatest shaman in the
world. How far, how wide? Across the strait and over
mountains. Down the mountains, far along the plains.
Where all plains end and deep pits spew from sunless dung
filled bellies men. Even so far and to the ends of all the earth,
I am the touchstone of all power that hovers round the
world. Hand closed – spirits sleep. Men's hearts lie at rest.
Hand open – air is filled with mysteries that terrorize the eye
and ear and thought of every mind. Throughout the world.
Of which I stand supreme. Only in my shaman's head the air
is clear. Only in my shaman's head the stream runs cool and

still and full. I shall know when you need me. You will find
me. Kwakiutl! Enough. That is all.

FOOL: Kwakiutl!

ALL: Kwakiutl!

FOOL: Quesalid!

ALL: Quesalid!

    (CARVER *goes*.)

FOOL: Kwakiutl!

ALL: Kwakiutl!

FOOL: Quesalid!

ALL: Quesalid!

    (*Great noise and clamour above which* KETTLE's *voice is heard*.)

KETTLE: Quesalid! O Quesalid! O Quesalid!

    (*Whistling off, turning gradually to bird-song*.)

SIX

Summer 1891.
Almost noon. Bird-song. CARVER *sitting at the side of a mountain
pool. He holds a western-style fishing rod with reel and tackle. He is
asleep.*

FOOL *comes on, stripped to the waist. He kneels and washes his face in
the water.*

CARVER: (*Asleep*) Go for it, Old Woman. (*Smacks his lips*.) Go on,
Old Man. (*Smacks his lips*.) Take it. Take it. (*Opens his eyes*.)
That's the best sized fish I've caught for years.

FOOL: What kind of swimmers live in a mountain pool?

CARVER: Little Flabby Skin in Mouth. Little Broken Jaw Bone.
You fish all day and catch a mouthful.

    (*They embrace*.)
You're tired, boy.

FOOL: It took a day to cross the strait. All morning to climb up
here. The path's almost grown over.

CARVER: Do you ever go out hunting now? No. Too busy. Look
at me. Fit. Strong. In the last six months I walked a
thousand miles. I'm forty-six. How many are coming up this
afternoon?

FOOL: Oh – later. Tell me about your travels.

CARVER: I'm expecting quite a crowd. It's been so long.

FOOL: Not so many.

CARVER: Ha ha ha. Tell me. Who?

> (KETTLE *comes on. She carries a child and bowls of food.*
> CARVER *moves away from* FOOL *and smacks his lips at the*
> *water.*)

KETTLE: When you spent twenty dollars on that rod you should
have bought the fish to catch as well.

CARVER: Your brother's here.

KETTLE: I know.

CARVER: So. I get second greeting.

KETTLE: This is Dancer's girl. Say hello to Great Uncle Fool.

FOOL: Her fists are curled so tight. She's squeezed out all the
blood.

KETTLE: He frightens her. Chi chi. Chi chi chi chi.

> (CARVER *has started eating.*)

There's still the healing floor to sweep before the patients
come.

CARVER: They like a bit of dirt.

KETTLE: It's white with droppings. She's swimming in sweat.
Poor little fish.

> (BETSY HUNT, *sitting on the side of the stage, cries.*)

Are you hungry? Come. I'll feed you. There's more if you
want to fetch it.

> (*She goes out.*)

CARVER: Bring it out!

> (*He waits until she is out of earshot.*)

Go on. Who's coming up?

FOOL: Weaver's daughter Seagull has a pain behind her ear.

CARVER: Right or left?

FOOL: Left.

> (CARVER *gives* FOOL *his bowl.*)

Squatter cut his finger in a fight. It won't heal.

CARVER: Right or left?

> (FOOL *takes a mouthful of food and puts the bowl down.*)

FOOL: How long since you rowed across the strait, boy?

CARVER: You send me everything I need.

FOOL: Fort Rupert's changed.

CARVER: Are the houses down? Are the paths dug up?

FOOL: The paths are where they were. They lead to different places now.

CARVER: Squatter's finger. Right or left?

FOOL: Right. Tell me about your travels, boy.

CARVER: Ha. The plains. The grasses. The soft, soft earth. Ha. (*He seems to draw information out of the air.*) Something is hiding in the darkness. What is it, boy?

FOOL: We need you.

CARVER: My people always need me. They know where I am.

FOOL: Carver.

CARVER: Boy?
   (*Silence.*)

FOOL: They've stopped the potlatch.

CARVER: (*Genuinely surprised*) Who?

FOOL: The white men.

CARVER: How?

FOOL: There hasn't been a potlatch since the snows. They broke the dances up with guns. I went to argue with them.

CARVER: Who?

FOOL: The missionary.

CARVER: No good, boy.

FOOL: Where were *you*? He listened. He said the white men think it's wrong to work all year to build up wealth to give away. I said we Indians think like this: Great Chief Father Sun smiles down on generosity and trust. He said he wished that that was so but Jesus Christ came down to earth to tell us life is hard. No man survives unless he keeps his riches to himself. And then he took me to another room and there – I swear, Carver, I swear that this is true – his family were potlatching. A pine tree standing on the floor. His children and his wife and brothers wearing coloured hats. The tables laid out for a feast. They're giving presents to each other. I asked: what happens if a person gets a present and doesn't give a present in return? He told me that would cause such sadness, people always give a present in return. I told him they were just like us. They give and take on the same day, we spread it through the year. That's all. You're potlatchers,

I said. You whites are Kwakiutl too. His brothers threw me out into the snow. Carver, boy, we need you.

CARVER: Yes?

FOOL: To argue with them.

CARVER: Ah.

FOOL: They've heard of you. They know you are the wisest of our men. If you say our potlatching is just as fine as theirs, they'll listen. But you must go soon. I am holding a potlatch next full moon.

CARVER: Can't it wait?

FOOL: Bear Face has his eye set on my place. He can trace the chief's place on his mother's side. If I hold a potlatch I will keep the place. I'm wealthier. But if I don't . . . The people think I'm old and weak. He's thirty-two. He'll win.

CARVER: You were chief at thirty-four. That's not so bad.

FOOL: I'll lose because I'm weak, but not because the white men tell me to. This is the first trap, boy. If we fall in they won't be satisfied until they suck our bones.

CARVER: If we fall in? Boy, I sat five years on this mountain top. On one side I see Indians sailing their canoes, fishing. I see hunters chasing through the forest after bears. I hear wolves howling in traps. I hear young people laughing in the darkness, crying sometimes. The lights of celebration shine up through the night. That's what I see on this side. And on the other – nothing. Emptiness. I mean the air. I thought: travellers come to see us with tales. White men are eating up the world. Why can I see nothing from my mountain top? I made new shoes. I went to see. I walked and walked. I didn't see one human face – white, red, black, any. Until I found a village. Boy, you think Fort Rupert is a village? No. A village is a place where white men drink and fuck and red men scrub the floor and sit in jail. Fort Rupert is a little piece of heaven. I asked one: boy, why don't you run off home? You're nothing but a pig to these white men and they won't make you fat before you die. Go home to your people, boy. He answers: my people are dead. The whites put fences round my land. Sometimes he pays me, then I eat. The more I work, the more I eat. Get out of my way and let me scrub

51

the street. Six months I walked and everywhere the same. Say I was unlucky. Say I only saw the worst. But even if the good is ten times more . . . That's why the east view of the mountain side is empty. If you want to see the people, look in their graves or in the white men's jail.

FOOL: You say don't talk to missionaries. Who then?

CARVER: Leave the missionaries to rot. The policemen are the one.

FOOL: You go to them. You see this all so clear. You argue with them.

CARVER: I don't know a way to set it straight.

FOOL: We have our guns.

CARVER: Ha ha ha ha. Shoot. The sunless pit from which the white men creep is very wide and very, very deep. They're aiming to destroy us, boy. If I leave this mountain top, go down and argue with the whites and lose, we're lost. I owe it to our people to stay strong. Who else is coming up this afternoon?

FOOL: Your strength is me. I tell you what you need to know to cure. A child could do the rest.

CARVER: If he has the power.

FOOL: Bear Face has his own shaman. He won't spy for you.

CARVER: I don't need chiefs. I don't need dreamers. I don't need spies. I say the words. I show the worm. And people live. That's enough for one lifetime.

(*Silence.*)

FOOL: Sea Front's wife won't work. She sits by the sea and stares at waves. Wolf Hunter has difficulty breathing. That happens every summer. Sh! Sh!

(*He takes the rod from* CARVER.)

Hey hey hey hey.

(*He pulls up a tiny little fish.*)

CARVER: I never worked out how you do that trick.

FOOL: No trick, boy. Or the best of all. Step in when all the work is done and bow to the applause. What is he?

CARVER: Flabby Skin in Mouth.

FOOL: Ha ha ha, Flabby Skin in Mouth. Ha. I'm so glad you could come. (*Intoning.*) Now, soul. Go back to the deep, bleak places where you live.

(*He hits the fish on the head with the rod.*)

CARVER: Don't hit so hard. You'll smash it flat.

(FOOL *looks at the fish.*)

FOOL: Spider Eye turned his ankle in a fight.

CARVER: Right or left?

FOOL: Left. That's all.

CARVER: In six months? Who died?

FOOL: Bee Eater.

CARVER: No more?

(FOOL *shakes his head. He throws the fish back into the pond.
Silence.*

DANCER *comes on. He wears Western clothes.* KETTLE *follows,
carrying the child and dragging a branch she uses as a broom.*)

Dancer!

(*They embrace.*)

I'm glad you came, boy. I'm so glad you came. Kettle, bring
him food.

KETTLE: He's eaten.

CARVER: Second greeting again.

DANCER: I rowed across with Fool.

CARVER: Dancer! Boy!

(*Delighted, he breaks his fishing rod and throws it down. He
stands beaming at* DANCER.)

Let me hold Sparrow.

DANCER: Betsy.

CARVER: Let me hold Sparrow.

KETTLE: You'll make her cry.

CARVER: She always says I make the children cry.

(*He takes the child.* BETSY HUNT *cries.* KETTLE *takes the child
back. The crying stops.*)

There's a secret way of holding them the women won't
reveal. Ha ha. So. What can you tell me? What have I missed
in the world?

DANCER: I came to fetch my girl and say goodbye.

CARVER: You're not going yet. I haven't seen you. Dancer.

(*He embraces him.*)

You'll have to wait for Fool to row you back. Boy? My

53

patients always stay at least one night. Secrets. Lurking. Secrets. (*To* DANCER) Sit. (*To* KETTLE) What haven't you told me?

KETTLE: I wanted to tell you. You get so angry. I pleaded with him to change his mind. He wouldn't listen. You wouldn't listen.

CARVER: (*To* DANCER) Where are you going?

(KETTLE *starts to go.*)

(*To* KETTLE) You can't run away from your life.

(KETTLE *stops,* BETSY HUNT *cries,* KETTLE *weeps, sits and plays with the child.* BETSY HUNT *gurgles and laughs.*)

KETTLE: (*Sings to the child*)

Baby rocked in his canoe.

Raise your spear and catch a fish.

Give his soul back to the sea.

Eat him any way you wish.

DANCER: (*Speaking over the singing*) I'm going south.

CARVER: That means for ever. How far?

DANCER: Codfish Bay. Where the Skokomish live.

CARVER: Why?

DANCER: Some white men there are studying our people.

CARVER: The Skokomish were never our people.

DANCER: They need a man who knows our tongue.

CARVER: White men study the Skokomish? Have their own people no secrets they can learn?

DANCER: I don't know who they are or why they've come or what they want. They pay a dollar a day.

CARVER: Are there no more fish in the sea? Are there no more deer on the mountains? Have the goats on the hills run away?

DANCER: We may not drink. We may not potlatch. We may not keep slaves. We may not marry who we choose. We may not leave our wives. Our chiefs may not carry guns. The missionaries don't treat our people well. Some boys have taken jobs in lumber camps. They help to tear our forests down. I won't do that. Some boys have taken jobs in boats and factories. They help to empty all the seas of fish. I won't do that. In my job I'll help the white men write about our lives. Our language. What we think. Don't try to stop me,

54

father. They chose me when I said I was a shaman's son.

CARVER: What do you know about a shaman's life?

DANCER: Everything.

CARVER: Ha ha. Ha ha ha ha. Everything. Hee hee hee hee. You couldn't cure a broken toe-nail, boy. Ha ha. Look. You have my eyes. The white man's jaws are clamped around our necks. I told Fool this. But there is no need to run. I'll teach you all my secrets. When white men cover the countryside like snow, we shamans will stand taller than the trees.

KETTLE: (*Sings*)

Baby rocked in wicker crib.
Who made this wicker crib for you?
If I teach you how to weave
You can rock your baby too.

DANCER: All the people know about the worm.

CARVER: You told them.

DANCER: Father – they told me. They knew the bullet shot at you was blank. Then it all came out.

CARVER: (*Stunned*) Was blank.

DANCER: (*Perceiving the truth*) You didn't know.

CARVER: (*To* FOOL) I'll slit your throat! (*To* DANCER) I didn't know! But people come to me for cure. They're climbing up the mountain now. Not all my people know.

DANCER: Not all. Some still believe. Those who you've cured believe.

CARVER: That's half Fort Rupert. A quarter of the island. I've cured the sick for twenty years.

DANCER: At any other time, the bullet – well, what's one deception when you've done so much? But now. The skies are open. Who knows what will fall? Fool's right. You must go down and argue with them now. Before you have no power left at all.

CARVER: I'll slit his throat!

DANCER: You can't heal gun wounds with a bloody worm.

CARVER: It's not the worm. It's me.

DANCER: You can't hold back diseases white men bring.

CARVER: I can. I do. There's no illness in the world I can't cure, boy. Believe me. Ha. This is your revenge. I knew. However

55

much I loved you I knew the time would come when you would turn on me for giving your place away. Stay with me, boy. The truest sign of strength is to forgive.

DANCER: So many of our men are dead, a one-eyed dog can hold a place.

KETTLE: (*Sings*)

Baby crying on my knee,
Baby scared and hungry too.
Don't cry, baby, don't you cry.
Your father will take care of you.

DANCER: For the past two years, father, Fool has paid people to put on sickness and row across the strait. He's struggling to hold his power too. When Bear Face is chief they won't come any more. I may not be home again for years. How will you live with no one to pay you fish and meat? Father!

(CARVER *has pushed a fish hook through his finger. He holds the finger up, his head dropped back.*)

CARVER: Don't touch me.

DANCER: (*To* KETTLE) The hook's caught in his finger. Bring a cloth.

CARVER: Don't touch me. I can cure myself. What I must decide is whether to let him take our grandchild. Does your wife share these beliefs?

(*To* KETTLE) You can look after it. It hates me. You can bring it up. Don't let him touch it. Kettle!

(DANCER *takes the child from* KETTLE.)

KETTLE: I can't. I can't.

DANCER: I'm going now.

(KETTLE *embraces him.*

BETSY HUNT *cries.*)

(*To* CARVER) Take Fool's advice. Go down. (*In tears*) Don't pull!

(CARVER *tears the hook out of his finger.*

DANCER *goes off.* BETSY HUNT *cries for a moment. Then stops.*

KETTLE *sweeps the ground.*)

CARVER: Did you know this?

KETTLE: He told me. Yes. I knew. You men! You useless, useless men!

56

(*She sweeps her way quickly out of sight.*)

CARVER: I mean the bullet! Did you know? Well, little
swimmers. Tiny as you are, it's your turn to feed me now.

FOOL: Will you come down?

CARVER: Seagull. A pain in her left ear. Squatter. Finger won't
heal. Spider Eye.

FOOL: Boy, answer yes or no. Will you come down?

CARVER: Spider Eye turned his ankle in a fight. Seagull. Pain in
her left ear. Dancer! Dancer! Dancer!

(*He runs off.*

FOOL *takes out his pistol and loads it. He looks out over the
landscape, stretches, wanders out.*)

BETSY HUNT: Our Great Chief Fool said: fire came down from
the sky. Fire carried our shaman off into the clouds. Our
shaman will return one day and drive the white man from
our land. That's what Fool said. And even if those people
didn't know the world is wider than Vancouver Island, in
our winter's night out in the cold, thinking that – it almost
kept me warm.

(*Towards the end of this speech,* KETTLE *comes on with a basket
of berries. She crushes them by rolling a stone over them, singing
softly to herself as she does so.*)

KETTLE: (*Sings*)

When I am grown I will bend and pick up clams.

When I am grown I'll pick berries all day long.

When I am grown I'll catch salmon in my nets.

When I am grown I'll catch whales and drag them home.

Sergeant Ola

For Michael Stewart

CHARACTERS

SERGEANT OLA
GAU
MORO, his wife
JOANA, his second wife
PIOBA, Moro's father
DON
MAKIS, a cargo leader
SCOVILL, the local district officer
MAMBA, a policeman
SWANSI, a policeman
YIM, a clerk in Port Moresby

The play takes place on the north coast of Papua New Guinea and in Port Moresby, 1945–52. There is an interval between scenes five and six.

Sergeant Ola was first performed at the Royal Court Theatre on 23 October 1979. The cast was as follows:

GAU	Ben Thomas
PIOBA	Bruce Alexander
MORO	Mia Soteriou
JOANA	Sarah Lam
SCOVILL	Will Knightley
OLA	Norman Beaton
MAMBA	Paul Kember
SWANSI	Burt Caesar
MAKIS	David Rintoul
DON	Jimmy Findley
YIM	Joseph Charles

Director	Max Stafford-Clark
Designer	Peter Hartwell
Lighting designer	Jack Raby
Music	Gaspar Lawal and Andy Roberts

ONE

The beach at Bogati, a village on the north coast of Papua New Guinea, 1945.
Bright sunshine.
A bare wooden table on the sand.
Loud sounds of the sea – waves breaking on the shore. Birds, crickets, etc.
Enter PIOBA. *He is fifty, short but strongly built. He wears traditional clothing, i.e. a laplap (a long waistcloth). He moves slowly, with a dogged and unthinking efficiency. The tasks he has to do he has done countless times before. He carries a brightly patterned beach umbrella and a green baize table cloth. He puts the cloth on the table and erects the umbrella.*
Enter GAU, *running, carrying a cardboard box. He is thirty, muscular, with a short straggly beard. He wears shorts and a vest. In* GAU, *nervousness and assertiveness are constantly at war. At the moment he is very excited and out of breath from running. This is not unusual for him and makes little impression on* PIOBA.
GAU *puts the box on the ground.*

GAU: You seen Moro?

PIOBA: In her garden.

GAU: I looked there.

PIOBA: In her house.

GAU: I looked. I got to find her quick time.

PIOBA: She'll come home by and by.

GAU: I got to find her now.
    (*He weighs the significance of what he is about to say, then says it as if in awe of the words.*)
    Cargo has come.
    (PIOBA *laughs.*)
    I been to Saidor village. In Saidor cargo's come.

PIOBA: What kind of cargo they got in Saidor?

GAU: Tinned food, bags of rice, steel tools, a cardboard box –

PIOBA: Tobacco?

GAU: I didn't hear about tobacco.

PIOBA: The only something I call cargo is tobacco. Ha ha ha.
    (*He finishes erecting the umbrella and starts to go out.*)
GAU: Cargo's come! It's come! I got to tell Moro. You seen Joana?
PIOBA: In her garden.
GAU: I looked there.
PIOBA: In her house.
    (*Exit PIOBA.*)
GAU: I looked. Moro! Joana! Moro! Cargo's come.
    (*He runs off.*
    Enter MORO. *She is thirty and wears traditional dress.*
    She walks down front to the shore and looks out, shading her eyes
    from the sun with her hand.
    Enter PIOBA *carrying a flagpole and a flag. He erects the*
    flagpole.)
PIOBA: Our new kiap's coming here today.
MORO: What for?
PIOBA: They don't tell me what for. They say: fix it. I do. They
    say his skin is so soft, soft. We got to hide it from our sun.
MORO: Why we got to care for wetmen, Papa? Is it friendly how
    they treat us? They sleep in big wood houses. We sit in the
    sand.
PIOBA: I am an old, old rooster. I love only two. Number one is
    you, my daughter. Number two: tobacco. One time people
    tell me: oh cargo's come to Mindiri. Next time: oh to Bongu.
    Ha ha ha. I been waiting so long for tobacco. Such a small,
    small pack tobacco. Now they say there's cargo in Saidor.
MORO: Cargo? In Saidor?
    (*She runs down to the shore and looks out to sea again.*)
PIOBA: Oh no.
MORO: It's come! Great ancestors! You've sent us cargo!
PIOBA: (*To himself*) Mouth, I got to have a good, strong talk to
    you.
MORO: Yes. It's come. It's come.
    (*Enter* JOANA. *She carries a box of taro roots.*)
JOANA: What you see there, Moro?
MORO: Cargo! Our ancestors sent us cargo!
JOANA: Where? I see nothing. Where's it?
MORO: There!

64

JOANA: Oh! Cargo! Cargo!

MORO: No, I got it wrong, girl.

JOANA: Cargo!

MORO: That's a rock.

JOANA: It's cargo. Ancestors are bringing cargo!

PIOBA: (*To* JOANA) It's a rock. Same dirty rock I stare at every day, all my life long. Our ancestors are parrots, see? Not fish. Those people in Saidor, their ancestors are fish. If they get cargo it will come by sea. But I'm not a fish. My daughter's not a fish. Gau is not a fish. I hope you're not a fish.

MORO: She's not a fish, Papa.

PIOBA: True. You're a bee. True?

JOANA: True.

MORO: Gau would never marry one of those fish.

PIOBA: If our ancestors send cargo, we get it through the air. Parrots and bees.

MORO: But cargo never comes through air, papa. It comes by sea.

JOANA: It comes for wetmen every day by sea.

MORO: Wetmen get it all. And we blackfellas?

JOANA: Nothing.

MORO: But I see why our cargo never comes. It's you. Cargo never comes while we work for those wetmen. Our ancestors hate them.

PIOBA: Hate? Our ancestors? Our sweet grey parrots? No. They love all the people – me, you, bees, wetmen, altogether. They even love those fish.

MORO: Then why won't it come?

(JOANA *has started scraping the taro.*)

JOANA: When you said cargo I thought: now I never got to scrape scrape scrape again.

(GAU *runs on.*)

GAU: Moro! Joana! I got the secret.

MORO: Which one?

GAU: This time I know true. It's no use to wait, wait, wait for cargo.

MORO: Then what?

GAU: You take it.

MORO: From where?

65

GAU: We wait here every day for cargo. True? But ships go to
      Saidor. So I went down the hillside to the harbour. There's a
      big ship – full of wetmen. All wetmen take, take, take, that
      cargo. My belly's sick with thinking: they got such great
      cargo. We stand empty. I hiccup, like this, see? (*He hiccups.*)
      So I ask a wetman: kiap, where's a cargo for me? He says:
      which one's your village? I tell him: Bogati. He says: here's
      the one. Take care. And so I brought it home!

MORO: You brought it home?

JOANA: What did you bring home?

GAU: Cargo! (*He goes to his box.*) Here!

MORO: That's it?

GAU: True.

MORO: No time!

GAU: True! This is just a small, small cargo, so it came in a
      wetman's ship. Soon our own ships will come.

JOANA: Cargo has come!

MORO: So – open it.

GAU: Now?

MORO: Go on.

GAU: Why not?

(GAU *starts to open the box, carefully at first, then he rips the
paper off and tears the sides open, crying:*)
Cargo! Cargo!

JOANA: ⎱
MORO: ⎰ Cargo! Cargo! Cargo!

(GAU *takes the following items from the box and sets them on the
ground. A cry of 'Cargo!' breaks from* GAU, JOANA *and* MORO
*with each new item: a hairbrush, a mirror on a stand, bottles of
tablets, a shaving brush, a Bible, a pair of pyjamas, a dressing
gown and other intimate accoutrements of the European male's
toilet.*

JOANA *uses the brush on her hair,* MORO *runs up and down
looking at herself in the mirror.*

GAU *puts on the pyjamas.*

PIOBA *approaches cautiously, opens the bottle of pills, tries
eating a few. They continue crying out: Cargo! Cargo! Cargo!*

66

Enter SERGEANT OLA *followed by District Officer* SCOVILL *and*
MAMBA *and* SWANSI *in policemen's uniform: khaki shorts and
shirts and peaked caps. They carry canes.*
OLA *is thirty-five. He wears the uniform of a sergeant in the
Royal Australian Forces.*
SCOVILL *is a fifty-year-old Australian professional
administrator. He wears very light, white clothing and
sunglasses. He is deferential and polite.*)

SCOVILL: Well, blow me down. They've got my shaving kit.

OLA: That's your box, kiap?

SCOVILL: My name, look – Theo Scovill.

(GAU, MORO *and* JOANA *are shocked – still and quiet.* PIOBA
immediately backs away to the safety of the flagpole.)
It got mislaid in Melbourne. How did these fellows get their
hands on it?

OLA: Pack up this new kiap's box.

GAU: (*To* SCOVILL, *from a distance*) This is *our* cargo, kiap.

OLA: This kiap can't speak the language, fella. Pack up all this
stuff.

MORO: Oh why do all these good, good things belong to wetmen?
Where are our good things?

OLA: Wait. You'll hear.

GAU: We heard that wait too many many times.

OLA: Pack up!

(GAU, MORO *and* JOANA *put the items back in the box.*
OLA *guides* SCOVILL *to the table.* SCOVILL *opens his shooting
stick and sits behind the table.*
OLA *stands beside him.*
SWANSI *and* MAMBA *stand at a distance on either side.*
GAU *puts the box in front of the table. He,* JOANA *and* MORO *go
and sit on the ground facing away from the table.*)
Flag!
(MAMBA *runs the Australian flag up the pole.*
SCOVILL *takes off his sunglasses, mops his forehead with a
handkerchief, gets out a piece of paper and begins to read.*
GAU, MORO *and* JOANA *ignore him.* SCOVILL *looks at* OLA.
OLA *knocks on the table.*

They ignore this too.)

SCOVILL: My dear friends belong me –

(*They ignore him.*

OLA *gestures to* MAMBA *and* SWANSI. *They advance towards*
JOANA, MORO *and* GAU *but without threatening them.*

GAU, MORO *and* JOANA *sigh deeply and turn to face* SCOVILL.

SCOVILL *reads.*)

Friends belong me. War i pinis nau. Dispela man (*points at*
OLA) i stap officer belong me. Dispela man i stap here in
village belong you. Dispela man bambai tok you how dispela
Bogati village belong you bambai stap mobeta. Mi savvy
dispela village is buggerap. Tasol, gavman tok dispela village
bambai stap gutpela village. Mi no tok bulsit. Mi tok tru.
(My friends. The war is over now. This man is my officer.
This man has come to your village. This man is going to tell
you (by and by) how your village Bogati will be improved. I
know this village has been damaged. However, the
government has decided that this village will soon be an
excellent village. I am not deceiving you. What I say is true.)
(OLA *comes forward.*)

OLA: This kiap tells you the war is over now. He says the
government will help you make Bogati village pretty good.
You got it?

GAU: The government said this long before war came.

MORO: Wetmen live in big wood houses. We still sit in the sand.

SCOVILL: (*Hesitantly*) Wat datpela toking? (What did that person
say?)

OLA: Dispela pipel no kan bilip houmas lucki i stap, kiap. (These
people can't believe how lucky they are, kiap.) People, I am
Sergeant Ola.

GAU:
MORO: } Ola.
PIOBA:
JOANA:

OLA: I am home from war. I come to tell you – Australians,
English and we blackfella soldiers beat up every Japanese.
Now there is no more war. So I am on a trip to every village
on this coast with my true friend, this Mr Scovill, your new

kiap. We come to bring a great big progress to the people.
You know what progress it?

JOANA: 'Progress'?

MORO: 'Progress'?

GAU: We never heard of 'progress'.

MORO: What is it?

OLA: You will hear. Now, people always tell us: one day their
ancestors will bring them riches, happiness. One day, one
day, that day belong cargo's sure to come.

GAU: That's true!

JOANA: That's true!

MORO: It will!

OLA: But when? Nobody knows. Now here is the first knowledge
that we bring you. Your ancestors will bring you nothing.

GAU:
MORO: }They will! They will!
JOANA:

PIOBA: Ancestors bring everything.

OLA: No, nothing! Today, last Thursday, in a year. So we tell
you: stop this longing for the cargo. You won't get it. No
time. Not at all. Olright. Now this is the true word. The
wetmen got some big big ancestors. Adam and Eve. (*To*
SCOVILL) True? Man bilong bipo i Adam an Eve? (The
ancestors – men belonging to the time before – are Adam and
Eve?)

SCOVILL: True! True!

OLA: True! Wetmen's ancestors are Adam and Eve.

JOANA:
PIOBA:
MORO: }Adam and Eve.
GAU:

OLA: These two are far more powerful than anyones we got. Now.
(JOANA, GAU *and* MORO *exchange anxious glances*.)
Do you people of Bogati want tinned food, knives, dresses,
electricity?

GAU:
MORO: }Yes, yes, we want, we want!
JOANA:

GAU: But we don't know the way to make it come.

OLA: Olright. Then I will teach you. Question number one. Can your ancestors bring you these things?

GAU: No.

JOANA: No.

MORO: You say no.

OLA: And I say true. So question number two. How can we get them?

(*Silence. More anxious glances.*)

From the wetmen! The wetmen got them. See? So if we want to get these things we got to live like wetmen tell us. We got to do just like they do. We got to make new houses in straight lines. We got to build new roads between. We got to keep our pigs in good strong sties outside the village. Houses must be tidy. Wash your hands with soap before you eat. Salute this famous flag. Is this true, kiap?

SCOVILL: True! It's true!

OLA: If you live just the same as wetmen, they'll give reward to you.

GAU: 'Reward'.

JOANA: 'Reward'.

OLA: So will you do it?

GAU:
JOANA: } Yes, yes! We'll do it! Yes – olright! We will!

OLA: In that way progress comes. You got it?

JOANA:
GAU: } Yes, yes! Progress! We got it! Progress! True!

SCOVILL: You pinis? (*Are you finished?*)

OLA: Pinis, kiap.

(SCOVILL *puts on his sunglasses and folds his shooting stick.*)

SCOVILL: Where would I be without you, sergeant?

OLA: Or us without you, kiap. We're such a team.

SCOVILL: I must get back to base. You can handle this place on your tod now, can't you?

OLA: True, kiap. On my tod.

SCOVILL: Press on.

(OLA *points at Scovill's box.* MAMBA *picks it up. Exit* SCOVILL *followed by* MAMBA *and* SWANSI.

PIOBA *begins to dismantle the flagpole and umbrella and to fold up the table cloth.*)

PIOBA: I've seen so many kiaps. English kiaps. America kiaps. Australia kiaps. Japanese kiaps. All come to New Guinea. All make big, big promises. One day, away they go. What we got? Nothing. Before those wetmen came here we were rich. So many parrots bright in the black trees. Now? Look at us. Will wetmen give us some good thing for nothing? Rubbish. Bullshit. Every bloody time.

OLA: Did you fight in the royal war, old man?

PIOBA: Not that one, no. Other battles. Not that one.

JOANA: He just lay in the sun.

GAU: He's just an old, old rooster, Ola.

OLA: Now this is the true history how I got my reward.

MORO: Listen, papa. These days you must learn about the world.

OLA: One day those wetmen told me: serve the English king. Kick all the Japanese out of your island. When that's done, you'll get a big reward. This was their promise. They promised this to me for all my fighting. Now just look at me. I'm working with the wetmen – side by side. The kiap and me – what a great team. Like man and wife. So close.

MORO: Ola, this reward – ?

OLA: Yes.

MORO: Is it cargo?

OLA: If you ask for cargo you get nothing. Why do you ask for it? Why?

MORO: We are rubbish people, Ola. We feel no bone inside our skin. Cargo isn't just nice dresses, tinned food. Cargo is –

OLA: What? What is cargo? You tell me.

MORO: I saw what came for wetmen in the war. One day they had nothing. Next day – so many guns. Cargo is something altogether strong.

OLA: Why do you want guns?

(MORO *can't answer.*)

Why? War is finished. Japanese are gone. If you build houses, dig latrines, forget to do that cargo, wetmen will give you reward the same as they gave me. And it will be so many, many things. Like these.

71

(*He takes these objects out of his kitbag.*)

(*To* MORO) Wetlady's knives. (*To* JOANA) And one for you.

(PIOBA *sits up.*)

(*To* GAU) This blade's for you to shave. See? Wetmen like smooth chins.

(OLA *throws a pack of tobacco to* PIOBA.)

Olright, old man?

(PIOBA *catches it. He stands, amazed.*)

PIOBA: Tobacco! It has come!

(OLA *holds up a Bible.*)

OLA: And this one is the best. You heard the wetmen read this Bible many times. True?

GAU: True.

MORO: True.

PIOBA: True.

JOANA: True.

OLA: Now you must learn to read with your own eyes. All wetmen's knowledge comes from inside here.

(*He gives the Bible to* GAU.)

This is a beginning, nothing more. Do what the wetmen say. Live like they do. Progress just has to come.

GAU:
JOANA:
PIOBA:
MORO: } Thank you, Ola. Thank you, Ola. Thank you.

OLA: Bring me some sweet, sweet drink.

(JOANA *pours liquid into a cup and takes it to* OLA.

MORO *starts chopping the taro roots.*

GAU *starts shaving in the bucket.*

PIOBA *rolls a cigarette, lights it by twirling a stick in a block of wood* (*an easy and speedy operation*) *and smokes – which makes him cough.*)

(*To* JOANA) Those palm trees play cool shadows on the grass. They're calling to us. Come.

JOANA: I can't, Ola.

OLA: I been a long time in the army all alone. Come with me now.

JOANA: I can't. I married Gau.

OLA: Gau's got a wife.

JOANA: I'm Gau's wife number two.

OLA: But that's not progress. One man, one wife. That's the wetmen's line. Kiap got a wife. I got to have one too. And you are too, too pretty.

JOANA: You talk so sweetly, Ola.

OLA: I've seen the girls of Brisbane. I choose you. (*To* GAU *and* MORO) This girl's going to take me for a walk. We're looking for a place to build a school. Come.

(*Exit* OLA *and* JOANA.)

MORO: Gau, look at this, Gau.

(*She chops the taro with her knife.*)

GAU: Cargo! No. Reward. That's it. Reward. We're going to get reward, Moro. We're going to do just like the wetmen do.

TWO

The beach at Bogati. Bright sun.

MORO, PIOBA, GAU *and* JOANA *are sitting round the table laid with tin plates, mugs, forks and spoons (no table cloth).*

A flagpole.

PIOBA *and* GAU *share a dinner suit.* PIOBA *wears the jacket and a laplap.* GAU *has the trousers, collar and tie. He is clean-shaven.*

MORO *wears a dress.* JOANA *wears a skirt to the knee and a blouse. All the clothes are tattered cast-offs.*

MORO *pours water into mugs for each of them. With great solemnity,* GAU *raises his mug in a toast.*

GAU: God savvy the king!

(*They all raise their mugs.*)

MORO:
JOANA: }We savvy him very good too.
PIOBA:

(*They clink the mugs together and throw the contents over their left shoulders.*)

JOANA: What now?

PIOBA: Now food.

MORO: Not food first.

PIOBA: No?

GAU: What now then?

MORO: I don't know. Think!

(*They think.*)

GAU: Flag. Raise the flag.

MORO: Not flag first.

GAU: No?

MORO: Not first.

JOANA: What then?

GAU: ⎫
MORO: ⎭ Think!

    (*They think.*)

PIOBA: I got it. Food!

MORO: It's reading!

GAU: Reading what?

MORO: Read that book Ola gave.

GAU: How can I read that book Ola gave?

PIOBA: He can't.

MORO: No?

GAU: I can't.

MORO: Then say it anyhow. You heard them read it many, many
    times.

GAU: I can't.

MORO: You can't.

GAU: I don't know what they say.

PIOBA: Olright. I had enough. (*He puts his mug down and walks
    away.*)

MORO: Papa!

PIOBA: This working makes my belly hungry. I need food.

MORO: We'll eat soon.

PIOBA: How soon?

MORO: Soon.

JOANA: You got to stay. See? There got to be four.

    (*She fetches him back to his seat. They think. At last:*)

GAU: I got it! Flag and reading at one time.

MORO: Can they do two things at one time?

GAU: I've seen.

MORO: (*To* PIOBA) True?

GAU: I've seen! I've seen!

JOANA: They never argue.

PIOBA: True.

74

MORO: True.

GAU: True.

MORO: Olright. Flag and reading.

PIOBA: Olright.

MORO: Stan' by – go!

> (PIOBA *goes to the flagpole and raises the flag of the New Guinea Yachting Club very quickly as* GAU *opens the Bible at random and recites rapidly:*)

GAU: 'In quick time, in twinkle, twinkle of my eye – trump, trump, trump, trump – for that trumpet will go too-oo-oot! Dead men walk one time more and we shall be so changeable. That's all!'

> (GAU *drops the book, dashes to one side and looks out. They wait expectantly.* GAU *comes back. He sits.*)

PIOBA: *Now* food?

> (*They all look at* MORO. *She thinks.*)

MORO: Olright. Now food.

> (JOANA *uncovers the food.*)

PIOBA: That's all?

GAU: They eat big suppers!

PIOBA: True! They eat big suppers! True!

MORO: It's all we got.

JOANA: We got no more.

GAU: It's not enough!

PIOBA: It's not enough!

GAU: We got to do it true!

> (*He hiccups.*
>
> PIOBA *walks away.*)

MORO: But this isn't true eating.

PIOBA: Not true?

MORO: It's all right if we don't eat plenty now.

GAU: It is?

MORO: Just so they think we do.

PIOBA: Who?

MORO: Adam and Eve. The wetmen's ancestors.

GAU: But how to make them *think* there's plenty food?

> (*They think.*)

MORO: We dish it out four times.

GAU: Adam and Eve will see us dish it out.

MORO: They won't know it's the same food.

ALL: That's it! You got it! True! True! True!
> (*They clap and bang the table.*
> PIOBA *rejoins the table.*
> GAU *dishes the food on to the four plates.*)

GAU: (*In a contrived voice*) 'Won't you try some? It's too, too sweet!'
> (PIOBA *bursts out laughing.*)
> Am I wrong?

MORO: Don't stop! Don't stop!
> (JOANA *is laughing.*)

GAU: 'And try a lick of this.'
> (*He laughs.*)

MORO: This is something serious! 'Try some of this. It's quite good I suppose. It's burnt with my own stove.'
> (*She has divided the plate of food between the four. They are all roaring with laughter.*)

JOANA: 'So kind of you to look inside our home.' True?

ALL: True! True! True!
> (JOANA *divides her food.*)

JOANA: 'Too dear, too dear, too dear.'

MORO: (*To* PIOBA) Now you.

PIOBA: There's just enough for me.

ALL SHOUT: Now you! Now you!
> (PIOBA *divides his plate of food between the four.*)

PIOBA: You've all got more than me.

MORO: (*Pointing up and whispering*) Sh! Sh! We all divided into four.

PIOBA: (*Whispering*) You've all got more than me!
> (GAU, MORO *and* JOANA *gesture upwards.*)

ALL: Sh! Sh!

PIOBA: Olright.

MORO: Now. Stan' by – go!
> (*They eat with forks and spoons. They start slowly then get faster and faster.* GAU *gobbles his down, dashes to one side and looks out.*)

JOANA: I'm still eating.

GAU: You hold it back. Quick! Eat!

76

(PIOBA *eats from Joana's plate and she stuffs the rest into her mouth.*)

MORO: It's gone.

(GAU *looks out. They wait on tenterhooks.* GAU *sits again.* MORO *thinks furiously.*)

Do singing! Sing!

(*She starts, they gradually join in.*)

God savvy our greasy king

God savvy our greasy king

God savvy our greasy king

God savvy our greasy king

God savvy our greasy king

God savvy our greasy king

God savvy our greasy king

(*While singing they look at* GAU. *He looks out to sea, leading them on. The singing ends.* GAU *hiccups. They face each other, tense and desperate.*)

GAU: (*To* MORO) What more?

(*They sit gloomily thinking.*)

PIOBA: Tring-tring. Tring-tring. Tring-tring. Tring-tring.

(*He looks round at the others acting innocent of the source of the sound, then picks up a mug and holds it to his ear as if it were a telephone receiver.*)

What the bloody hell? Who you think you're talking to, you monkey face? What's that, you stinky fool? It's coming! It's coming! It's coming!

(MORO, JOANA *and* GAU *rise up from the table and dash to where* GAU *observes the sea, staring out.*

PIOBA *is left on the chair, mug pressed to his ear.*)

JOANA: Where?

MORO: Where?

GAU: Ask where!

PIOBA: Where is this ship, you halfbake brute? I see. It isn't coming yet. We must do it again.

GAU: Again?

PIOBA: Especially eat. We got to eat again.

(*They return to the table.*)

MORO: I got it! There's always someone else to give them food.

Joana, give the food.

JOANA: We ate it all.

PIOBA: Get more.

JOANA: From where?

MORO: My cousin's got a box of fish.

GAU: Steal your cousin's fish?

PIOBA: Borrow her cousin's fish.

GAU: Her cousin never lends his fish.

PIOBA: They said we got to eat.

MORO: Cargo *will* come for my cousin too. It's what we got to do!
(*They all look at* GAU.)

GAU: I'll steal your cousin's fish.
(*He goes out.*
They sit on the ground, agitated and expectant.
JOANA *bursts into tears.*)

JOANA: Adam and Eve will know it's stolen fish. Our ships will
never come.

MORO: Cry! You cry! I won't die the rubbish I was born. It's got
to come. For me.
(*They wait.*
Enter GAU *carrying a cardboard box.*)

GAU: They steal from us. We steal from ourselves. Here. Your
cousin's fish.
(*He holds out the box.*
No one moves.
MORO *goes to the flagpole, quickly lowers the flag half-way and
puts a corner of the flag inside each ear. She speaks very quickly,
in a whisper at first, rising to a shout.*)

MORO: Holy father, holy father – we are with you, we are with
you. God of Isaac, Jackass, Abegnigo. Bless us, bless us –
once in the name of the holy ghostly, twice in the name of
your mama Maria, three times two make sixty-six, three
times three make ninety-nine, you will not gut your fish on
the admin. house front step! – oh father, oh father.

ALL: Oh father! Oh father!

MORO: Where shall we find life?

ALL: It will be found in the glorious paradise.

MORO: Where shall we find hope?

78

ALL: We shall find it in the kingdom of the meek.

MORO: I hear it. It will come. Joana – servant! Give my cousin's fish. Quick! Eat!

(*They scrabble back round the table.*

JOANA *serves them food. They eat, shovelling the food into their mouths with their hands.*

MAMBA *and* SWANSI *rush in.*

MAMBA *pushes the table over.* SWANSI *pulls down the flagpole, destroys it, folds up the flag.*

All this happens very quickly. The four stand together aghast.)

MAMBA: This is a strike!

GAU: It's work!

MORO: It's work!

SWANSI: This is a strike!

PIOBA: Dogs? Who says we are dogs?

MAMBA: If this is work, who pays you?

MORO: This is a kind of work like wetmen do.

PIOBA: We are not dogs!

MAMBA: You are workers from the plantation.

SWANSI: You must go back to work on the plantation.

(MAMBA *is hitting* GAU *with a cane.*)

MORO: We're working here.

JOANA: It's work! It's work!

(SWANSI *is threatening* PIOBA *and* JOANA *with his cane.*)

PIOBA: We are not bloody dogs!

(SCOVILL *dashes on. He carries a notebook in which he looks up words.*)

SCOVILL: Stapim! Stapim! (Stop! Stop!)

(*The policemen stand to attention.*)

We are not savages! Mi skool you stapim (*Looks up word*) pantomime, no – lunacy, ah! (*He's found it*) me skool you stapim longlong, not mek these pipel dai! (I ordered you to stop this madness, not to kill these people.)

MAMBA: They wouldn't stop.

SWANSI: True, kiap, they wouldn't stop.

(JOANA *is lying on the ground.* SCOVILL *goes to her.*)

SCOVILL: Pathetic creature. (*To* MAMBA *and* SWANSI) These are your mit and blut. They're mit and blut belong you.

(GAU *rises up as if possessed*.)

GAU: You wetmen have everything. Why? Look at me. Dirty. Black.

SCOVILL: What's in this bottle?

MORO: It's water, that's all.

(MAMBA *sniffs the bottle*.)

GAU: I am a fine man! I am a good man! (*Hiccup*.)

SCOVILL: He's drunk. This man (*Looks it up*) is longlong wiski.

GAU: Why do you wetmen make us feel like dogs? Why? I got to find out now.

(*He is shaking violently*.)

SCOVILL: Hopeless. Longlong long wiski.

(*He gestures to* MAMBA, *who takes hold of* GAU.)

JOANA: We only do like you do, kiap. That's all.

MORO: ⎫
PIOBA: ⎭ That's all. That's all.

SCOVILL: My friends. My good dear prens belong me. Me tingtink you like prens. We were on ol rot long progress – taim behind. Nau – lukim you. The same as wilpela animals. Me savvy you no laik the good tings belong you, but savvy well! – you ken get good pay on plantations. (My friends. My good dear friends. I think of you as friends. We were on the road to progress – the future. Now, look at you. Like wild animals. I know you don't like the material possessions you have but you know well you can get good pay on the plantation belonging to the mission station.)

JOANA: We hate plantations!

GAU: Oh we hate plantations!

SCOVILL: Prayer got a place, but hard work got one too.

MORO: We don't see you work work for what you get.

SCOVILL: You pray your labours will be blessed with fruit. Good, good. But fruit will never rain down prom ol sky.

GAU: (*Still as if possessed*) We don't want fruit. We got fruit. We want tins of meat. Uh! Uh!

SCOVILL: We don't want to use ol power belong us to hurt you.

PIOBA: We don't want hurting. No no no.

(*He starts to cry*.)

SCOVILL: I have your interests deep, deep in my . . . (*Looks it up*,

80

puts his hand on his heart) klok.
(JOANA *bursts into tears.*)

JOANA: We only tried to see if it would work! We only tried to see!
(*She weeps and weeps.*
SWANSI *bursts into tears.*
GAU *bursts into tears.*)

GAU: Oh help us! We are poor blackfellas! Teach us how to get
reward! (*He falls on his knees before* SCOVILL.)

SWANSI: Give us reward! Give us reward!
(PIOBA *and* SWANSI *kneel and weep.*)

SCOVILL: (*To* MAMBA) Reward? What's this reward?
(MAMBA *bursts into tears.*)

SWANSI:
MAMBA:
GAU: } Reward! Reward! Reward! Reward!
JOANA:
(*Enter* OLA.)

SCOVILL: (*To* GAU) No, no, old pren. We pinis with that now.
(*He tries to lift* GAU *up.*)
You are not slaves! You no are slaves! But if you want good
things you got to work. Work on our plantation. We'll give
you plenty pay.
(GAU *resists* SCOVILL's *attempts to lift him.*)

GAU: Pay! Pay! We want our pay!
(*The weeping bursts out anew. Only* MORO *is dry eyed.*)

SWANSI: Pay!

MAMBA: Pay!

JOANA: Pay!

GAU: Pay! Teach us the way to get our pay!

SCOVILL: What is this? Anarchy? What this is? Anarchy or what?
(MORO *bursts into tears.*
OLA *comes forward.*)

OLA: What, rain in all your eyes? You natives of my heart, why
can't you see? Obedience is what marks out the man. Shout
at a pig. She still tears down your fence. Who cares?
Tomorrow she will wake up in your stew. But man wants to
be here, tomorrow, always, every day. So he must learn to do
new things. If Mr Scovill tells you – work on his plantation,

81

brothers, sisters, do it. Follow the wetmen's line. Blow
with the strongest wind like rainclouds do. We want a sunny
sky.

JOANA: Then will our good things come?

SCOVILL: Nothing comes from nothing. Understand? If you
work, we'll pay.

OLA: Now go home. Go on. Home.

(MORO, PIOBA, GAU *and* JOANA *take off their clothes and throw
them on the ground forming a pile. They all have traditional
clothing under their borrowed attire.*

MORO *and* GAU *go out.* JOANA *starts to go with them.*)

Joana! This place has too much mess. So clean it!

(JOANA *collects the utensils, clothing etc. lying on the ground.*)

SCOVILL: It's no good, chum. I'll ask Port Moresby to send a
supervisor. Someone who understands these people, knows
what makes them tick. Damned if I do.

OLA: Kiap, I know these people.

SCOVILL: Damned if I don't. That's my lot. How's that?

OLA: Kiap, I know these people. Truly well.

SCOVILL: You told me you could stop this cargo nonsense. I gave
you a free hand. You failed. There's no shame, sergeant, but
the job has to be done. And soon.

OLA: I was up the coast. Your orders, kiap.

SCOVILL: These – pantomimes don't only happen here. They
happen up and down the coast. True?

OLA: True, kiap.

SCOVILL: You've had simply no effect at all. Too bad. You
seemed to show such promise when you came.

OLA: I don't show promise, kiap. Those people in Brisbane, they
showed me promises.

SCOVILL: Now don't take it to heart. In normal circumstances
you're first rate. Number one. But folks are getting jumpy.
Not only the plantation bosses, either. See my problem?
This nonsense must be stamped out. Quick time. Perhaps if
you'd received administrative training –

OLA: Me? I'm Sergeant Ola. I've been trained.

SCOVILL: That's fine in wartime, chum. But these people aren't
soldiers. You need to take a different line with them.

OLA: Which line is this one, kiap?

SCOVILL: Learn to do it our way, forcefully, or I'll have to get white supervisors in.

OLA: Look. Somewhere hides the worst mistake of all. Can you tell, kiap? No. Everything, so peaceful. Sky and sand and sea. Joana, it is you.

(JOANA *turns amazed*.)

Her husband has two wives. How often does the church say this is wrong?

SCOVILL: Indeed. It's wrong.

OLA: Do Australian people do it?

SCOVILL: No. Wrong.

OLA: You hold back our progress. Understand?

JOANA: Last night you did such sweet sweet talking, Ola. Why are you so hard today?

OLA: Gau and his wife, that's good strong stock. You are a thirsty, creeping vine, crawling round their roots to suck them dry. This is the one bad crime we still commit and I am saying clearly – it must stop. You got to leave that Gau.

JOANA: Must I leave Gau, kiap?

SCOVILL: I'm afraid, my dear – yes. True.

(JOANA *bursts into tears*.)

JOANA: It's me who holds back progress. Our cargo never comes because of me.

(*She runs off*.)

OLA: See how shamed she is? She runs away. Ha ha. Kiap, I can teach these people. We don't need white supervisors here. Leave this whole place to me.

SCOVILL: How good's your writing?

OLA: Not too much of writing.

SCOVILL: Reading?

OLA: No, kiap.

SCOVILL: See? We need white supervisors just to write reports. Don't look downcast. Press on.

(*Exit* SCOVILL.)

OLA: A native man of promises, that's me. Before war came, during the war, after the war, now, tomorrow, next week, next year, when I die. A native man of promises – that's all. I

made no promise, kiap, but I heard promises in Brisbane
with these ears. Wetmen played humbug with us, laid us
down beneath a tree, talked sweet, so sweet, took pleasure
and slipped in the seed. Seeds grow. We're heavy with your
promise now and something very soon got to be born.

(MAMBA *and* SWANSI *have been standing some distance away,
observing.*

*They are in their early twenties, jealous of their authority, full of
bluff aggressiveness and swagger. Their loyalty is ultimately to
their status. As this has been conferred on them by wetmen they
are far from sure how permanent it is and what they need to do to
retain it.*

(*To* SWANSI) You are a reading, writing man?

MAMBA: Him? No. He knows nothing.

OLA: I got to find a reading, writing man (*To* MAMBA) Are you?

SWANSI: Him? No time. He knows less than me.

OLA: And you two are police?

MAMBA: True.

SWANSI: True.

OLA: Oh no. Policemen would have stopped the cargo bullshit
here while I was fighting it way up the coast. I came back.
Four streams of water flowing from your eyes into that sea of
ignorance. Ho ho. I think police believe in any bullshit
thing.

MAMBA: It's true!

SWANSI: We do.

MAMBA: We got to.

SWANSI: We're police.

OLA: Could you believe –

(OLA *stops, thinks about this, decides to risk it.*)

Could you believe I was a kiap?

(MAMBA *and* SWANSI *burst out laughing.*)

MAMBA: No time. Kiaps are wetmen.

SWANSI: Blackfellas can't be kiaps.

OLA: And when our rewards come?

SWANSI: (*In awe*) No one can say now what will happen then.

MAMBA: No one can say.

OLA: We'll all be kiaps then. Got it? You, him, me.

(MAMBA *laughs*.)

SWANSI: Me?

(MAMBA *stops laughing*.)

I'll be kiap?

OLA: All will be kiaps.

(SWANSI *and* MAMBA *look uneasily at each other*.)

Mr Scovill wants to get wetmen policemen. He told me.
Then what's the good of you? But follow me and I will make
you kiaps. True? Where did Joana go?

(*Suddenly both* MAMBA *and* SWANSI *are filled with energy*.)

SWANSI: Into the bush.

MAMBA: Along the road.

OLA: Find her. A kiap must have a wife.

MAMBA: We'll go.

SWANSI: We'll find her, kiap.

OLA: Press on.

(MAMBA *and* SWANSI *run off*.
The table has been left lying on its side.

OLA *lifts it up so it rests on one corner and spins it on this corner
walking around it. After a moment he begins to recite, still
spinning the table*.)

In the beginning of our life, God made the world. The world
is one big testicle. He hangs up in the sky and turns himself
one time each day. One time, one time each day.

(*He stands the table on its legs and climbs on top of it*.)

I don't need your training, kiap. I will stop this cargo
bullshit. I will be forceful with these people. But I say keep
your promises. We're stuck here on this island same as you.

(*He lies down*.)

When will our progress come?

(*He stares at the sky*.)

THREE

*The jungle. Moonlight. Deep bird hootings. Crickets cheep and whir.
Enter* JOANA.

GAU: (*Calling, off*) Joana! Joana!

JOANA: Call Moro, Gau. Not me. It's wrong for men to have two wives. I stop our progress coming. If I leave it will come.

GAU: (*Calling, off*) Joana!

JOANA: (*Calls*) I'm Adam and Eve's good lady now. I won't lie
in your bed.

MORO: (*Calling, off*) Joana!

JOANA: No, Moro. Don't find me. I keep you in the sand.
Progress must come. Moon, you are women's guide. Ah no!
Wicked blackfella woman. Cut your face out, moon. Adam
and Eve will comfort me.

MORO: (*Calling, further off*) Joana!

JOANA: But how can I go home? How will my father
understand? He has three wives. I'll live wild in the jungle
like the bees. Oh!

(*She has seen* MAKIS *who has been standing in the shadows. He
is dressed in elaborate traditional ceremonial costume. He carries
a small sack.*

MAKIS *is one of the handful of cargo prophets who preached the
coming of the millenium to the peoples of Melanesia at this time.
Some rose and disappeared within weeks, some lasted months
and some whose promises coincided very precisely with the
aspirations of their followers remained authoritative and
respected for years. Their promises in essence were of a reversal
of the existent unsatisfactory social relations and the restoration
of dignity to a confused and humiliated people. The means by
which this material improvement was to be achieved were
entirely mystical.*)

Who are you?

MAKIS: This jungle is my jungle. Why do you leave your village?
What do you seek in me?

JOANA: I've nowhere else to go.

(MAKIS *empties his sack on to the ground. Many small metal
objects fall out. He holds these up as he describes them.*)

MAKIS: Nail. Screw. To make the house. (*A hinge which he opens
and closes.*) This one makes the door. (*A small canister of
oil.*) This one makes doors sing. (*A piece of bread.*) Inside
the house – a bread. Touch. Touch, touch!

(*She does and draws her hand back in shock.*)

Touch good! Touch!
(*He presses the bread into her hand. He takes her arm and makes her hold it up.*)
True! Like a gun! Cargo belongs to *our* ancestors! Not to wetmen!
(JOANA *has let her hand drop.*)
Hold it up! Up! Up! Cargo belongs to *our* ancestors. True!
JOANA: But Ola told us –
MAKIS: Ola? Ha ha. He tells all the people work for wetmen. Ha ha. I know, I know. But you'll get nothing.
(*He grasps her wrist and pulls her towards him.*)
You suffer hard, like all our people. True?
JOANA: Your heart!
MAKIS: My heart beats like a thunder. True! I have strong blood.
(*He cocks his head at various angles at her like a hen.*)
The wetmen say our ancestors are weak and theirs are strong. Why? The wetmen stole our ancestors!
JOANA: Stole them? Where are they?
MAKIS: In heaven. They lie in chains! They bleed!
JOANA: We must free them.
MAKIS: How? How to free them? How?
JOANA: We'll all go up to heaven when we die.
MAMBA:
SWANSI: } (*Calling, off*) Joana! Joana!
(MAKIS *waits until they have passed.*)
MAKIS: Go to heaven, daughter. Go now. All cargo in this land belongs to us. Set our ancestors free.
(*He gathers up his bits of metal and drops them in his sack.*)
Go to heaven. Go.
GAU: (*Shouting in the distance*) Joana! Joana!
MAKIS: I am Makis! I am the open road.
(MAKIS *vanishes into the shadows.*)
MORO: (*Shouting in the distance*) Joana! Joana!
JOANA: All cargo in this land belongs to us. Only me of all our people know this secret. Don't worry, Gau. I'll make cargo come.
MORO: (*Further away*) Joana!

GAU: (*Far away*) Joana!
(*Loud sound of the sea.*)

FOUR

The beach at Bogati. Morning. Soft sound of the sea. The table. At one side a pigsty, three foot high with a lean-to door. Enter PIOBA *pulling a rope. He wears shorts and a vest. A pig is attached to the unseen end.* PIOBA *is half-way across the stage when the pig refuses to go any further.* PIOBA *tugs the rope.*

PIOBA: Hurry up, Mr Truman. I built you a good new pigsty house just like Ola said. Time to move in. Mr Truman! (*He tugs the rope. Mr Truman grunts and squeals.*) Get your nose out of that pool! You hear me? Kiap says Mr Truman is a good, good man. I gave you a famous name. Does Mr Truman stand up to his knees in shit? It took six days to build that house. So come now.
(*He pulls hard but Mr Truman won't move.*)
Olright. You want to live in that house where your papa lived and where his papa lived.
(*He tugs the rope. Mr Truman grunts and squeals but refuses to move.*)
Did I knock your old pigsty down? No. When cargo comes you'll go back home. We'll all go home. We'll stop this rubbish. Got it? Olright. Let's go.
(*He walks on but the rope draws taut as Mr Truman refuses to move. He tugs the rope.*
DON *runs on. He is twenty-five. He wears shorts and a shirt. He is short, wiry, emotional, energetic.*)

DON: Where can I find Sergeant Ola?
PIOBA: Where you come from?
DON: Mindiri. You know where he is?
PIOBA: You got tobacco?
DON: Can you say where Sergeant Ola is?
PIOBA: Clear out my road. I got work with this big head pig.
(*He tugs the rope.*)
Come, come!
(*Mr Truman grunts and squeals.*

88

DON *takes a small pack of tobacco from his pocket and gives*
PIOBA *some.*
PIOBA *rolls it immediately.*)
The answer's no. Nobody here seen Ola for a week.
DON: I heard he's in Bogati. I must find him.
PIOBA: You going to talk long?
DON: I got to find him now.
PIOBA: Olright. You talk. I'll tie my old pig here.
(*He ties the rope to the leg of the table.*)
DON: If you see Ola tell him Don says: go to Mindiri. We need to
hear the story he tells there.
(*Exit* DON, *running.*
The table begins to move as Mr Truman goes home.)
PIOBA: Hey! You long long pig! If Bogati's not straight in quick
time, wetmen give us no pay.
(*He grabs hold of the table and stands in the middle of it.*
Enter GAU *and* MORO.)
Gau and Moro work hard hard on plantation. I built up this
house. So do your bit, old pig.
(GAU *and* MORO *sit, exhausted.*)
GAU: Is Joana home?
PIOBA: Not yet.
GAU: And our reward?
PIOBA: Not yet. I'll also have a rest. Mr Truman, man, you wear
me out!
(PIOBA *lies down on the table, his head against a leg, smoking*
and coughing.)
MORO: This is the wrong work, Gau.
GAU: I know.
MORO: Wetmen never work so hard to get their cargo.
GAU: I know. But which one is the right work?
MORO: I don't know.
(PIOBA *coughs.* MORO *looks up at the sky.*)
You see that? Eagle of the night. Papa, did you see it?
(PIOBA *is asleep.*)
Now there'll be a storm.
(*Enter* OLA *and* SCOVILL *further down the beach.*)
OLA: See how good these people have been working, kiap? Look

89

how many huts are planted in straight lines. How many
streets run (*Gestures with his arm – a straight line*) down to the
sea. How many pigsties stand proud in the grass. How many
latrines dug deep in the earth. The men and women work on
your plantation. Oh my! If a big man from Brisbane came
here, he'd be surprised. He'd think he was back home. Ho
ho. Brisbane looks just like this place. I've seen. Could you
make them do this work? No, kiap. White supervisors? No.
You had to wait for me.

(MORO *comes down the beach to* OLA. GAU *follows.*)

MORO: Ola! Joana's lost.

OLA: Sh, woman. Not that now.

GAU: Joana's lost!

OLA: She went home to her village. That is all.

GAU: No one has seen her face for six days now.

OLA: Kiap, I'll give you a picture of the way I teach the people.
(*He leads* MORO *and* GAU *away from* SCOVILL.)
Olright. Now. Listen. Joana knows it's wrong to be a man's
wife number two. You got it?

GAU: Why, Ola?

MORO: Why? I need a second woman in the house.

OLA: It's wetman's law. One man can't marry two. Soon I'll go to
her village, bring her home and she will marry me.

GAU: She's not in her village, Ola. We searched every thicket,
every cave. She's gone for good.

OLA: I told you she will be my wife. Now go on home.

MORO: We've done everything you tell us. What we got?

GAU: Raw hands, sore backs. That's all. We'll look one time more
along the beach.

MORO: Ola – that reward, it must come soon.
(*Exit* MORO *and* GAU.)

OLA: You see, kiap? That's the way I bring the peace here,
everytime.

SCOVILL: Sergeant, you've done superb work in this village.
Bogati is a model of its kind. But elsewhere on this coast it's
cargo, cargo, cargo. Confess, now.

OLA: What must I say?

SCOVILL: Is it true?

90

OLA: It's true.

SCOVILL: Now, in Port Moresby Admin. runs a special training course for natives with ability. You've proved you have that. We want to use you further, expand your work with us. You're going on that course.

OLA: Did you run on this course, kiap?

SCOVILL: Me? Oh no. It's just for native fellas.

OLA: Oh. Just for black buggers. I see.

SCOVILL: Sergeant – do I ever use those words?

OLA: Kiap, can't you see we're loyal? True, we are. But people are not stones. They got to know. When will it come?

SCOVILL: What?

OLA: Their reward.

SCOVILL: But what reward *is* this?
(OLA *is surprised by this.*)

OLA: You don't know, kiap?

SCOVILL: No!

OLA: But it's easy. It's only what the army promised me.

SCOVILL: Oh – progress. Is that what you mean?

OLA: True! Progress! That's it! Progress!

SCOVILL: As long as these folk keep on working, progress – well – it comes of its own accord.

OLA: Oh true, kiap. We know that. It just comes on its own. But kiap, they're asking, when?
(*Enter* DON. *He stands and watches.*)

SCOVILL: Your plane leaves for Port Moresby in the morning. Eight o'clock. Training starts in two days' time.

OLA: Will I be trained by blackfellas like me or by wetmen like you?

SCOVILL: Believe me, chum, I've simply no idea. One thing. Find out what's happened to that girl, Joana. I've had reports of three girls drowned this week. All second wives. One would be natural. But three? Everything those people do becomes an epidemic. Press on.
(*Exit* SCOVILL.)

OLA: But we did every last damn thing you say, you lying kiap. You know every word about reward.

DON: Sergeant Ola. I looked for you everywhere. I ran so fast I

fell two times. I'm cut, look, here and here. You got to come
to Mindiri.

OLA: I can't talk. I got thinking to do.

DON: In Mindiri the wetmen buy our gardens. They pay whisky
or a pair of shoes. I hear you say cargo will never come. If
wetmen buy our gardens and we never get our cargo, Mindiri
is nothing. One plantation and one church. That's all. You
got to come and tell us what to do.

OLA: I don't *know* what to do! I got no words for you Mindiri
people. Bugger off! Go home!

DON: But will our cargo come?

OLA: If someone asks me this just one time more, I'll think it's
true what wetmen say, that blackfellas got cabbage in their
heads. I'm saying, saying always the bloody same. I fought in
the war. You got it? They promised goods to me. You got it?
If we follow the wetmen's line we'll get those goods. You got it?

DON: No.

OLA: People in Bogati got it. Why the damn hell can't you get it?

DON: Adam and Eve are wetmen's ancestors. True?

OLA: I brought you this knowledge.

DON: And they send ships to wetmen. Have I got it?

OLA: Now you got it well.

DON: But wetmen tell us Adam and Eve are our ancestors too.

OLA: This is old, old knowledge. Look – I understand these
things. Go home. Say what I always say: 'Just work. Reward
will come.'

DON: No. Listen! Adam and Eve send cargo to the wetmen but
they're our ancestors too. If they send cargo ships to wetmen
why don't we get them as well?

OLA: They never send us ships!

DON: But why? Why, Ola? Why? I got to know.

OLA: Go home! Go back to Mindiri! You waste my time. Only
wetmen can get cargo.

(DON *is almost crying with frustration and rage*.)

DON: But why don't we get our own cargo, if Adam and Eve are
our ancestors too?

OLA: Because we're rubbish! See? They never send us cargo
because we're rubbish blackfellas. We're shit. Even to our

92

own ancestors we're nothing but black buggars. Oh it's true!

DON: (*Crying*) We got to get it, ola. They'll take all our gardens. We got to get ours too.

(OLA *holds* DON.)

OLA: We'll get our own. I promise you. We'll get it. What's your name?

DON: Don.

OLA: Olright, Don. I'll find the way. We'll get it. Wait and see.

DON: We can't wait long. We're sick men till you come.

(*He starts walking off.*)

OLA: Are you a reading, writing man?

DON: Three years at mission school.

OLA: Did you learn to write reports?

DON: I did.

OLA: And reading circulars?

DON: My reading's pretty good.

OLA: Olright. You stay in Bogati. I found my secretary.

(*Thunder some distance away.* MAMBA *and* SWANSI *enter, running. They wear shorts and shirts – not uniform. They stand staring at* OLA, *panting.*)

SWANSI: Ola!

MAMBA: Ola!

SWANSI: She's found!

MAMBA: Joana's found!

OLA: You two are not in policeman's clothes. Why's that?

SWANSI: We left wetmen's police. We follow you.

MAMBA: We're your two boss boys now.

OLA: Olright. Now's the time for changes in Bogati.

SWANSI: But kiap, Gau found Joana.

MAMBA: True! Joana's found.

(*Enter* GAU *bearing* JOANA'*s drowned body. Also his Bible.* MORO *follows.*)

OLA: Joana!

(DON *lays* JOANA'*s body down.*)

GAU: I looked along the misty shore. I found clams and crabs and green snail shells, a parrot fish, an octopus and her.

(*Thunder nearer.*)

Earthquake! Run, run. No. It's in my head.

(MORO *takes* JOANA's *head in her hands.*
PIOBA *gets off his table and goes to look at* JOANA.)
(*To* OLA) She learnt your lesson well. Salt water cleaned her teeth. The surf washed out her hair. She's smart as a wetlady now. I got only one wife now like wetmen tell us. Has it come? Ola? Has our reward come?

OLA: I could say many things. Who knows what they are? A sweet woman is dead. That's all. This is my secretary. We will find the way to make our progress come.

MORO: Speak all day, Ola. We won't hear a word. We followed every line you gave. We're finished with you now.

OLA: I'm going to Port Moresby. Flying. In a plane. I'll find out why we never get our progress.

SWANSI: Yes, find out. Find out why.

OLA: I'll find out why these damn, damn wetmen treat us like dry shit.

MAMBA: Come back and tell us, Ola.

OLA: I will come back.

SWANSI: You got to.

MAMBA: Oh you got to.

OLA: That time – that lovely, easy time I told to you – in Port Moresby I'll find ways to make it come.

SWANSI:
MAMBA: } We know you will, Ola. We know.

(*Tears are running down their faces.*)

OLA: Joana. Sweet, sweet, girl. I'll say goodbye to you. (*To* DON) We got work. Off we go.

(*Exit* OLA, *followed by* DON, MAMBA *and* SWANSI.
Thunder. Rain starts to fall.
GAU *picks up the Bible. He opens it at random and recites.*)

GAU: 'Their bellies won't be hungry. No no no. They won't be thirsty anymore. The sun will be so gentle on their skin. For the little sheep will give them juice and wipe the water far, far from their eye.'

(*He tears the Bible in half and stands with a piece in each hand.*)
The work we do is wrong! What is the proper work?

MORO: One day we will do everything exactly right. And it will

94

come.

GAU: What is the proper work like wetmen do? I got to know!

MORO: It will come, Gau. But it won't be tins of meat or
electricity that comes. Oh no! It will be guns.

FIVE

*An office in Port Moresby. Very bare. A filing cabinet. Two chairs.
No table. A picture of King George VI.*

YIM *is thirty-five years old and immaculately dressed. He wears khaki
shorts, an open-necked, sleeveless white shirt and sandals. He has a
clip-board.*

OLA *wears a brightly coloured shirt over his uniform, sunglasses and a
large straw hat. He has two large carrier bags.*

YIM: My first job in Port Moresby was teaboy. They told me:
'Something in this place is called saucer. Something that
stands on top of it is cup.' One day I spilled something called
tea out of the cup. It fell into the saucer underneath. My boss
threw all three somethings at my chest. Ho ho ho. But it
hurt. In those days I didn't wear something we call a shirt.
One day he said: 'Sort out the inward from the outward
telegrams.' I didn't dare to say I didn't know those words. I
studied the papers for hours. Inward. Outward. What does it
mean? At last I put the clean ones in one pile, the crumpled
in another. My boss explained. Inwards. He points to
himself. Outwards. He points away. I thought he means
those ones for me, these ones for you. I took mine home and
pinned them on the wall. Ha ha. There was a stink, oh
naturally. Confusion! Inwards – outwards. Dirty – clean.
This way I learned to see the wetman's world and started my
slow climb towards this job. Olright. We got five things to
see left on this list.

OLA: I go home in two days.

YIM: We have to choose.

OLA: Don't choose. I have to see it all. A thousand eyes watch
everything I see. This morning was another number one day.
I walk through the streets of Port Moresby, peep in

95

windows, go through doors. 'Good morning. How is your mother? How's your wife?' They answer me! Ho ho. I am so happy here. I must confess, all my cash is gone. (*He takes a kettle from a carrier bag.*) I bought this at the factory you showed me. Strong and lasting.

YIM: You've seen the engineers' training centre –

OLA: Got it.

YIM: The agricultural station –

OLA: True.

YIM: The saw-mill –

OLA: Oh I loved the saw-mill. Very handy.

YIM: The medical school –

OLA: That was not my best. Must we go there again?

YIM: The electrical power station.

OLA: Electricity! Oh I like that one.

YIM: The natural history museum.

OLA: Oh that one was like being back at home. So many of our ancestors locked in a cage. Why do they lock them in a cage?

YIM: Ancestors are from the old time. You don't need them now.

OLA: But why do wetmen want our old ancestors?

YIM: I think today the education training college.

OLA: You think? Mr Yim, take a tip from me. We leaders must be sure. Now I ask you a question. What am I?

YIM: What are you?

OLA: What am I? I am leader of my people. I look out for my people in so many kinds of ways. I try to bring them progress. Now I got to get an answer. What am I? A member of the Australian Admin. staff?

YIM: Not that.

OLA: I know. Not that. I know. Maybe a part-time number two helping to teach the people?

YIM: Well –

OLA: Not part-time. I know. I'm working, working, working the whole day. So what am I? Perhaps there is no answer?

YIM: Yes. There is.

OLA: There is?

YIM: There was a plan for you to hear it at a special briefing session –

OLA: A special one?

YIM: But as we'll get no work done till you know – an administrative post has been created specially for you.

OLA: Why specially for me?

YIM: Don't say I told you. Olright? (*Reads.*) 'In view of your qualities of leadership and your usefulness to the government, and now you have completed three weeks training, you have been awarded a salary of £4 every month. You will continue your education work. Your special post will have the title: native overseer.'

OLA: My special post.

YIM: That's right.

OLA: Does Mr Scovill have a special post?

YIM: Ha ha. Ambitious. His job needs certain qualifications.

OLA: I have a secretary. His name is Don. Every qualification I fall down, this Don is pretty good.

YIM: There is fifteen shillings a month for your number two.

OLA: Two of us are still too weak to fill one wetman's shoe?

YIM: Olright, Ola. Don't push too far. The education training office.

OLA: Two of us – like you and me – are still too weak?
   (*He waits for an answer.*)
   Who says I got to have a special post?

YIM: I don't know. Not me.

OLA: Who says? (*Pointing to the portrait*) That king?

YIM: Yes. Yes, he says. That king gives all the orders.

OLA: That king chose me?
   (*He considers this, smiles to himself, is partially placated.*)
   Olright. I got one more question.

YIM: It's my job to answer useful questions.

OLA: For three weeks this one has been waiting to come out. Now I am overseer it is time. When will our reward come?

YIM: Reward? For what?
   (OLA *holds up his carrier bags.*)

OLA: I am overseer of my people. This is our number one time. Tell them: don't wait another day. Keep your promise. Send us the reward.

YIM: What promise is that?

(OLA *takes off his sunglasses*.)

OLA: Building materials, tools, electric light. Progress!

YIM: That would cost a million pounds.

OLA: They promised it to me.

(*He takes off his hat*.)

Join the army. Kill the Japanese. When will reward come?

YIM: When you can pay. Not one minute before.

OLA: I see now how it is to be a beast trapped in a cage. Fish bite our nets to live. I've seen a pig caught in a trap chew off his foot just to be free. Bite off my head. Chew out my thoughts. What did I fight the war for? Mr Yim, what for? What did we build the houses for? Pigsties? Latrines? My people – they sit by the shore, wash their feet in an empty sea, swallow their little piece of fish, waiting, waiting. I can carry kettles home. But trucks? Boats? Foolish old crow. Wetmen are only men. Of course they lie. Throw away those dreams.

(*He pushes the carrier bags away*.)

YIM: Can I speak in confidence?

OLA: Let us talk man to man, says crocodile to fish.

YIM: It is my work to help you people. This is inside talk. Olright? In ten or fifteen years New Guinea may be given independence. You know what that means?

OLA: Is it electricity?

YIM: No.

OLA: Then it's not for me.

YIM: New Guinea belongs to Australia. They will make your country free.

OLA: You give us nothing now. In fifteen years we get nothing again.

YIM: We'll give you all the help we can afford.

OLA: Olright, kiap. Don't say more. Government has let my people down. Now I must know. What is the secret way to make the cargo come?

YIM: Do you believe that? No!

OLA: Adam and Eve send cargo to the wetmen. All the people know. I got to find that secret wetmen's way to make it come.

(YIM *picks up a kettle*.)

98

YIM: I took you to a factory. You saw them make these things.

OLA: I saw the factory way. That way takes weeks. First get the iron, then the steel. It is weeks and weeks! When war came to New Guinea, guns and ships and planes came in one day. Your job is helping people, true. Tell me that secret way. (*He leaps at* YIM *and holds him down by the throat.*) What makes cargo come?

YIM: Help! Help!

OLA: What makes it come? (*He lets* YIM *go.*)

YIM: You come down from the mountains. Dirty. Vicious. Fingernails like knives. Blood in your eyes. It took me nine years working every day to get this job. I tell you, son, the Bible isn't all that we believe.

OLA: How's that?

YIM: Push a wetman on the ground – he'd cut your savage throat.

OLA: Who doesn't believe the Bible? Kiap, who doesn't believe the Bible?

YIM: I'm sick of your damn questions. What's it now?

OLA: If wetmen don't believe the Bible, then who made the world?

YIM: Ola –

OLA: Who made *them*?

YIM: They don't know.

OLA: Don't they want to find out? Ha ha. Course they do.

YIM: I read in a book some wetmen say they are the sons of apes.

OLA: Of apes?

YIM: Of monkeys.

OLA: Wait. Wait, kiap, wait. Wetmen believe their ancestors are monkeys?

YIM: I read it in a book.

OLA: But that's what *we* believe. My ancestors are parrots. What are yours?

YIM: Adam and Eve.

OLA: (*Sure of his argument, with force and anger*) Who were your ancestors *before* the wetmen came?

YIM: Adam and Eve! Adam and Eve! (*He cries out – one long unarticulated cry*) Aaaaaah! (*And then – with great shame*) My ancestors are ducks.

99

OLA: You see? This is what *we* believe! Wetmen make us pray to
rubbish – Adam and Eve – while they pray to monkeys.
Monkeys send them cargo. And us? Our ancestors – our
parrots, bees and ducks – gave us our own good, happy times
before the wetmen came. They gave us these two jokers,
Adam and Eve, so blackfellas will stay more poor than them.
Olright! Olright and okeydoke! Wetmen won't keep their
promises. Monkeys won't send us cargo. I give it all away.
(*He upturns the two carrier bags full of kettles and scatters them
about. He overturns and destroys everything in the office except
the picture of the king which he takes off the wall and keeps hold
of. He tears his clothes off down to his laplap.*
YIM *watches dejectedly.*)
This shit is not for us. Our hearts are torn and sore from
wanting wetmen's things. I give them up! Progress –
goodbye! Once I was Sergeant Ola. Now I am native
overseer, chosen by this king. Blackfellas – here I come. But
I'm not empty-handed – no. I bring you a gift that has no
price, no electricity. Ha ha! I bring you back your ancestors!
I bring you back your own good times before the wetmen
came! Open your arms wide, my brothers. We're finished
with crying to be wetmen! I will bring you – you!

SIX

*The Coast – East of Bogati. Soft sound of the sea – waves breaking on
the shore.*
MORO *and* GAU *are both wearing simple items of European clothing.*
GAU *is scratching about in a box. To one side stands a large metal
drum, behind it a block of wood. Pieces of newspaper lie round it on
the ground. There is one piece of newspaper on top of the drum.*)
MORO: How long have we been working on this land now?
Digging it and digging it. Growing taro, growing sago. How
many years of working have we given this old earth? Each
year since I can remember. True, Gau? Every bloody one.
Since we went back to doing cargo, we got plenty work to
make it come. We got no time to dig this earth. For just one
year we leave this earth to lie. And what grows? Nothing.

GAU: We got food for one more day.

MORO: No more?

(*She looks out to sea, shading her eyes with her hand.*)

It won't come in one day.

(*She goes to look in the box. Finding nothing, she sits on the box.*)

We've done this cargo work for seven weeks now. What we got, Gau? Hungry bellies. Bleeding fingers. Nothing.

GAU: Maybe we should go back to plantation. (*Hiccup.*)

MORO: No time. This is our work.

GAU: Then we got food to go on working cargo.

MORO: I won't give up this work.

GAU: Olright. Eat stones.

MORO: Do wetmen go work on plantation? No! Do they eat stones? No! We got to go on.

(*She goes and sits on the block of wood behind the drum.*)

You truly sure this is what wetmen do?

GAU: We watched so close, close through that window. You saw too.

MORO: They do so many things.

GAU: I know their work. I know their play. This one is work.

MORO: They got more than one work, Gau. Everybody got more than one work. Does this one bring them cargo?

GAU: You give up?

MORO: (*Immediately*) No!

GAU: How long have wetmen done this work?

MORO: I don't know, Gau. For years?

GAU: And how long have we done it?

MORO: Seven weeks. Olright. Let's try again.

(GAU *goes to stand to one side of the drum.*)

GAU: Stan' by – go!

(MORO *starts beating out a rhythm on the drum with occasional high-pitched vocal accompaniments. She is imitating the sound and action of a typist.*

Meanwhile GAU *stands to one side, one arm behind his back. He paces up and down as if dictating to* MORO.)

We got five crates of sago here. It's time you sent a ship. Come bloody quick. The market, he is falling – something,

something. Oh yes. Dear Sir, in answering your – what was it? Dear Mister Thompson. Dear Sir or Missus Tree. Dear Reverend, we got six crates of copra here. It's time you sent us cargo. Your brother, Mister Gau. Dear – who's it? – Mister Pete. Come bloody quick. The market, he is falling – something –

(MORO *stops typing*.)

MORO: This one's done.

(GAU *takes the piece of newspaper off the drum, puts it on the ground, replaces it with another piece from the ground and* MORO *starts again*.)

GAU: Dear Mister Peter, we got five crates of sago here –

(PIOBA *runs on. He wears traditional dress and carries a gong made from an old shell case. He calls out loudly, banging his gong*.)

PIOBA: Throw out your missionaries! Praise your own ancestors!

MORO: Papa!

PIOBA: Ola says, forget wetmen's ancestors! Praise your own!

MORO: His head's so full of Ola talk he can't tell who I am.

GAU: It's your own daughter – Moro.

PIOBA: I know you. Two thieving crows. You gobble all the people's fruit and leave your shit on stones. Ola's bringing back the old, old time. So many parrots bright in the black trees.

(*He coughs and can't go on*.)

MORO: Papa! You're too old. And sick.

PIOBA: Just my inside is sick. Not me. Now I will kick this down.

(*He runs at the drum and tries to kick it over*. GAU *stops him. They grapple*, PIOBA *coughs and coughs*. GAU *lets him go*. MORO *goes to* PIOBA.)

MORO: Sit, Papa.

(PIOBA *sits on the wooden block*.)

PIOBA: Only I remember all the world before the wetmen came. So I am one big man with Ola. I travel there, here, here, there, up and down. I bang my bell. I tell the people: Who wants wetmen? No one. See?

(*Enter* OLA, *followed by* DON, *both in traditional dress*. OLA *wears the portrait of the king on his back*. DON *writes down everything he says in a notebook*.)

Throw up your ancestors! Don't do your missionaries! Ola!
These two are working cargo, kiap. What must we do?

OLA: We got to wake them up! For years we blackfellas were
sleeping. We dreamed such pretty dreams. Now, I, Ola,
native overseer, come from Gumbi. There we tell the people:

OLA: ⎫Forget wetmen! Forget cargo! Take back your gardens!
DON: ⎭Take back your old lives!

OLA: Now in Gumbi eyes are open. You are still asleep.

OLA: ⎫
DON: ⎬Wake up!
PIOBA: ⎭

(PIOBA *bangs the gong twice*.)
Wake up!
(*Gong. Gong.*)
Give it up or trial!

GAU: Only a kiap can hold a trial.

OLA: I am a kiap. I am overseer of a great part of the world. This
king of England gave my job to me.

OLA: ⎫
DON: ⎬Wake up!
PIOBA: ⎭

(*Gong. Gong.*)
Wake up!
(*Gong. Gong.*)
Give it up or trial!

GAU: Last time you gave us orders it was: follow wetmen's law.
Only one wife.

MORO: Which law do you teach now?

OLA: The truth about our lives here on this earth.

MORO: Which truth is this one?

DON: Listen! He will tell you.

(OLA *takes up a stance to make a speech*.)

OLA: When this old man was young, the world was lived in by us
blackfellas alone. Ah! What a time! No need to labour then.
Ripe coconuts bounce on a stone, crack, husk here, sweet
white meat there, milk draining on a leaf curled out below.
Then fish was still our friend, swimming up, offering his life
for us to eat. That time is gone. Why? Do you know? We

103

have forgotten our true ancestors. Parrots. Bees. Our ancestors are powerful and good. Our crops have never been so rich, our trees so high, our girls so warm, our penises so hard, our lives so full of happiness since that bad day we wanted wetmen's things. (*To* DON) So kick this rubbish down.

(DON *examines the drum.* GAU *defends it.*)

DON: How will this work bring cargo?

MORO: *We* don't know.

GAU: Don't kick it down. (*Hiccup*) We try to find the proper work!

DON: How does it work?

MORO: We hit that drum.

DON: Why?

MORO: It's what wetmen do. Why, Gau?

GAU: I say: 'We got five crates of sago here.'
I say: 'You send a ship.' Then put newspaper on and – something . . .

DON: Where is five crates of sago?

GAU: Which one?

DON: You say: 'We got five crates of sago.' Where is it?

MORO: We haven't got it. Or we'd eat it.

GAU: They don't *ask* for sago when they come. They bring us – I don't know! (*Shouting.*) What is it? What is the secret way? (*Hiccup.*)

DON: (*Laughs. Turns to* OLA) We don't need a trial here. They don't know what they do. If you say you got sago, Gau, you got to have it. See? I learnt this in mission school.

GAU: You got to have it first.
(*He thinks about this.*)

OLA: Kick that rubbish down.
(DON *knocks over the drum and tears up the newspaper.*)

GAU: You got to have it first!

OLA: Go home! Your ancestors are there. They'll care for you.
(GAU *and* MORO *go.*)

OLA: Don, go to Saidor. Tell Scovill that I'm doing pretty good. I stop the cargo and I teach my own line. Two jobs with just one head.

(DON *runs off*.)
To Bogati! The open road leads there.
PIOBA: Forget wetmen! Praise your own ancestors!
Forget wetmen! Praise your own ancestors!
(OLA *and* PIOBA *go*.)

SEVEN

Near the Administrative Building at Saidor.
A small plot of land marked out with four stakes connected with new
white rope – Scovill's flower garden.
SCOVILL is inside the rope, dressed in casual clothes, trousers rolled
up, sun hat. He is pruning flowers.
Outside the rope are two ornate wicker chairs. On one, a glass of beer.
MAMBA and SWANSI come on. They are out of uniform, in shorts and
vests. They stand outside the rope, behind SCOVILL's back, where he
can't see them, shuffling their feet nervously, trying to catch SCOVILL's
attention without disturbing him.
SWANSI pretends to catch a flying insect by clapping his palms
together.
SCOVILL leaps round.
SCOVILL: Jesus God! Who's there?
(*He falls to his knees due to the speed of his turn, clambers up,*
leans on the rope which gives way, leans on a stake, panting
heavily.)
Stupid buggers. Oh. You two. I thought they'd got their
hands on guns. Just a moment. Catch my breath, Pulim
wind belong me.
SWANSI: We hear Ola is home.
SCOVILL: That's right.
SWANSI: So where is he?
SCOVILL: Don't you use that impudent tone with me. You're
lucky I don't slap you both in jail. You're deserters from the
police force.
MAMBA: We want to ask a question, kiap.
SCOVILL: Can't it wait? This is my first afternoon off duty for a
month.
SWANSI: We got to talk to Ola, kiap.

105

MAMBA: We got to find him. He's nowhere. Kiap, help us.
    Please.
SCOVILL: I believe he's in Bogati.
    (MAMBA *and* SWANSI *look at each other in surprise.*)
MAMBA: Not here at your Admin. building?
SCOVILL: No. That all?
    (*He waits for an answer, then goes back to gardening.* MAMBA
    and SWANSI *hover.*)
SWANSI: Is this all the land they left you, kiap? Ha ha ha ha.
    (SWANSI *and* MAMBA *laugh.*)
SCOVILL: What the devil's going on?
MAMBA: We not laughing at you, kiap.
SCOVILL: No?
SWANSI: Oh no. We know too strongly how it feels. When we left
    your police we went home to our village Gomuru. All our
    gardens – gone. The wetmen left a small, small piece of us –
    just like they left for you.
SCOVILL: This is my flower garden! Look! Marigolds! Petunias!
    The wild dog rose!
MAMBA: (*Sympathetically*) True, kiap. It's wrong to leave a man
    with land so bad only rubbish plants will grow.
SWANSI: Don't worry, kiap. When Ola's king of this whole island
    you'll get your land back too – the same as we.
MAMBA: We got to find him. We looked all through kiap's house.
    He isn't there.
SCOVILL: You've looked all through my house?
    (*Enter* DON. *He wears shorts and a shirt.*)
MAMBA: All through!
SWANSI: Ola's kiap now so he lives in kiap's house. True?
MAMBA: We found your missis there. We think she must be Ola's
    missus now. True?
SCOVILL: Don! Come here. Tell these blighters what Ola's
    position in this district is.
DON: Native overseer.
MAMBA: We know that!
SWANSI: We know!
MAMBA: Ola's kiap now.
SWANSI: Cargo's come.

106

DON: No.
      (MAMBA *and* SWANSI *look at each other anxiously – then speak with confidence*.)
SWANSI: Cargo's come! We heard in Gomuru!
DON: There is no cargo for blackfellas. Ola says.
      (MAMBA *and* SWANSI – *as above*.)
MAMBA: } We heard!
SWANSI: } We heard!
SCOVILL: Then you heard wrong. You got it?
DON: Ola says cargo belongs only to wetmen.
SWANSI: But Makis says –
SCOVILL: Makis? What do you know about Makis?
MAMBA: Him? He knows nothing.
SCOVILL: And you?
SWANSI: Him? No time. He knows less than me.
SCOVILL: Are you followers of Makis or of Ola?
SWANSI: Ola.
MAMBA: Ola.
SWANSI: Everytime.
SCOVILL: Then turn round, go back to Gomuru and tell your
      friends the truth you heard from Don. Say Sergeant Ola's
      home. He's native overseer now. But nothing else has
      changed. Press on.
      (SWANSI *and* MAMBA *move to one side*.)
DON: Ola sent me for his orders, kiap.
SCOVILL: Right. Get your pencil out. There's been more trouble
      in Gumbi. They beat up the missionary and threw him out.
      Tell the sergeant – this one's serious. Something big. He
      must go to Gumbi. I want a full report. I must have names.
      It's Makis sure as eggs is eggs. He's dangerous and bonkers
      with it. Bonkers. Longlong. Longlonglong, I reckon. He's
      not the only one. In the western district three of those
      buggers sit in jail. Three. How many have we cornered?
DON: None, kiap.
SCOVILL: I rely on Sergeant Ola to put that right. The penalty for
      all cargo leaders is jail. Got that?
DON: Yes, kiap.
SCOVILL: Look at them. Bite my head off, given half a chance.

(*To* MAMBA *and* SWANSI) I told you two to scram.

DON: I'll make sure they go, kiap.

SCOVILL: Bless you.

> (DON *goes to* MAMBA *and* SWANSI – *out of* SCOVILL'*s earshot.*
> SCOVILL *goes back to gardening.*)

SWANSI: Tell us true now.

MAMBA: He can't hear.

SWANSI: What does Ola say?

MAMBA: When will it come?

DON: I told you true. Ola says there's no cargo for us.

> (MAMBA *and* SWANSI *look at each other anxiously, take this in*
> *and speak dispiritedly.*)

SWANSI: We gave up our job to follow Ola.

MAMBA: We got nothing now.

SWANSI: He got to bring us something.

MAMBA: What can we do now?

DON: Do as kiap says. Go home.

MAMBA: We got no home.

SWANSI: Wetmen took our gardens.

MAMBA: We got nothing there.

DON: Do as kiap says. Go home – and when you get there take
your gardens back. Ola tells you true: we'll get no cargo.
Instead we'll get our old lives back again. Go home. Close
down the mission school. Don't burn it. Just tell the kids
they got no need to go. Never, never work on their
plantations. Never answer questions. When they ask you:
who's your sister's husband? How many pigs you got? You
look like this. Jaw hangs down. Like this, see? They say,
'You bloody monkey face'! That's good. Then they go home.
You savvy this new line?

SWANSI: Take our gardens back!

MAMBA: And work them! True! We savvy!

SWANSI: True!

DON: Tell your people: 'Forget Makis and cargo.' Then go to
Bogati. You'll find Ola there.

SCOVILL: Don – pass my drink, good chap.

> (DON *hands* SCOVILL *his beer.*)

What are you telling them?

DON: I'm telling them: 'Go home.' (*To* SWANSI *and* MAMBA) Go
   home! Do what kiap says. Go home!
   (MAMBA *and* SWANSI *run out*.)
   You see?
SCOVILL: One day I'll get through to them. I swear I will. I'll
   drink to that.
   (*While he does, behind his back,* DON *sits on one of the wicker
   chairs, leans back and closes his eyes.*
   Darkness.
   The sound of bullroarers being whirled. MAKIS *appears in the
   darkness.*)
MAKIS: You ask me: why does cargo never come? I tell you why.
   Our ancestors see all good things we have. Houses. Pigs. So
   many good things. I tell you: break all those things down!
   Destroy your pigs! Tear down your houses! Our ancestors
   must see we got nothing. They must see how much we need
   them. Oh we need them. When we got nothing in our hands
   – ancestors will come home. Destroy! Destroy! Cargo will
   come!
   (*Then darkness again and the disembodied roar.*)

EIGHT

*The beach at Bogati. Late afternoon. The sun continues to sink
throughout the scene.*
*Pioba's pigsty has been partly destroyed – the door torn off and lying
on the ground, some of the panels splintered etc. The back section
remains intact. Broken pieces of wood are scattered round it, some in a
small pile.*
DON is inspecting the ruined pigsty and taking notes.
OLA: You think you know this earth, Don? True? You think you
   know this island? No. I flew home from Port Moresby. I saw
   it from the sky. You see gardens, fields, plantations. I saw
   green. Our green. I got to teach our people to see again just
   green. How many followers I got now?
   (DON *looks for the relevant page in his notebook*.)
DON: Not so many.
OLA: Who?

DON: That old man. Your two bossboys. Me.

OLA: Let me see that page. What's all these names? I'm just a poor old pig who never learnt to read but I can see there's more than four names here.

DON: They're crossed out.

OLA: Why'd you cross them out? You want to ruin me, Don?

DON: They were your followers. They follow Makis now.

OLA: Makis. Always Makis.Under every tree. Washed up with every wave. The people love him. Why?

DON: He tells them he'll bring cargo.

OLA: Tie up your mouth, Don. Tie it up! I ask the old men: 'Friends, tell me the spells to make food grow.' They answer: 'No. We've forgotten. We don't need them now.' I say: 'We do. We got to have those spells.' They say: 'But why? Cargo will come.' No no no no! So three months go. I stand here – big, big leader of this island, loved by Mr Scovill, chosen by this king and who've I got for followers? One sick old man, two longlong ex-police boys. Who else? You. And Makis?

DON: Seven thousand followers.

OLA: Who asked you? Tie your mouth up, Don. Tie it up. Seven thousand?

(*Enter* PIOBA.)

PIOBA: Mr Truman's dead. Nobody ate her. She's rotting in the grass. Why did they bugger up my poor old pig? Oh! Mr Truman's pigsty. You wild boys – here's my throat. I'm weak as Mr Truman. When I'm rotting in the grass beside my pig, who'll remember our old world?

(*He leans back against the remnants of the pigsty. Enter* MAMBA, *running. He salutes* OLA. OLA *looks away.*)

DON: Tell me your history.

MAMBA: I've been in Gorima. It's just the same as here. Every house pulled down, every pig dead.

OLA: And are those people happy when they've pulled down everything?

MAMBA: Who can say, kiap?

OLA: Happiness is so easy to tell. Sadness you can hide. And anger. Oh I hide them every day. But happiness is too

strong. It breaks free. Do Gorima people smile? Dance?
Sing?

MAMBA: They do.

OLA: I'm sick of this new living since that war. Bring back the
Japanese! This island's too damn foolish.

DON: You can't give up this work, kiap. It's too good. Maybe
years and years will pass before the people hear. You got to
go on talking, teaching what you know is true. This is our
power – only this – we know cargo won't come.

OLA: And what do I tell Scovill? Wait, years and years and years?
Seven thousand followers! It's no good, no good.

DON: Ola – !

OLA: Look Don, you get your fifteen shillings every month. They
don't care if you say nothing. You've talked three months'
worth in one day. Now pack it in.

DON: You changed my life. You made me see this whole world
new. You showed me this truth. Oh kiap, you know this
great, great truth so well you can't see what it means. If we
want our good life we got to build it up ourselves. I see it.
And I love what I see.

(OLA *is in tears*.)

OLA: Tell the people cargo's bullshit. Who believes you? No one.
Why? Easy. It isn't true. I've been to Brisbane, Don. I've
seen. The cars, the streets, the houses. Beautiful. I can't lie
anymore. Cargo is beautiful. That's why the people follow
Makis. True.

(*Enter* SWANSI, *running. He salutes* OLA.)

SWANSI: I been in Matoko.

OLA: Houses down. Pigs dead. True?

SWANSI: True. It's Makis.

OLA: Makis, Makis. Everytime. Swansi, Mamba – search the
jungle, where the worms crawl, where the snakes hide. Find
him. Bring him here.

DON: Ola –

OLA: I told you boys to go.

DON: First let me speak.

OLA: I give the line. You write it down. Boys, go!

DON: It's too soon to fight Makis. He has the strength of all those

111

followers. What have you got? Look – in my village there's no gardens left at all now. By winter time they'll all be weak with hungriness. Makis will be an old, old memory. They will follow you.

OLA: You see your village growing poorer, losing gardens. You feel nothing. I am overseer. I feel my people's sadness.

DON: Your people will dance! They'll sing!

(OLA *snatches Don's notebook and pencil from him. He breaks the pencil in half and throws it away.*)

OLA: Ah ha! I got it. You worry I'll make Makis secretary. Who knows? Maybe in the lovely time to come we won't need reading, writing any more. Go, boys. Wait. Don worries if you hear one word of Makis, you run from me. True, Don? Take earth, block up your ears. Don't hear a word he speaks. (*He hands them bits of earth. They block their ears.*)
Can you hear me?

SWANSI: (*Shakes his head*) No.

OLA: Take more.

(SWANSI *puts more earth in his ears.*)
But Don still fears he'll trick you through your eye. True, Don? (*He tears strips off the edge of Don's laplap*) So cover them. (*He binds their eyes.*)

MAMBA: How can we find Makis in the darkness?

SWANSI: How can we find Makis in the night?

OLA: Who knows where Makis hides? Follow heel and toe. You'll find him. Go.

(*He gives each of them a push. They stagger about.* SWANSI *staggers off.* MAMBA *bumps into* DON.)

MAMBA: Tell me where is Makis?

DON: We'll lose these boys, Ola! Then we'll be three.

(OLA *points* MAMBA *and pushes him.* MAMBA *staggers about and bumps into* PIOBA.)

MAMBA: Tell me where is Makis?

(PIOBA *points him in another direction.* MAMBA *staggers on. Then he stops, turns, makes for the pigsty and bangs his fists on it.*)
Tell me where is Makis! Makis! Makis!

(*The pigsty creaks and* MAKIS *crawls out, dragging his sack behind him.*

MAMBA *goes to him, touches him, pulls his blindfold off, sees*
MAKIS *and goes quickly to* OLA.)
My fist found him, kiap.
(MAKIS *empties his sack on to the ground. He holds up the objects
as he describes them.*)

MAKIS: Coffee bean. Cocoa bean. Peanut. Rice. Then comes – (*A
hinge which he opens and closes*) door. Inside – who knows?
You threw a pebble in a lake of spit. The ripples washed my
village. So I came. The mountains echoed: Ola! Saviour!
Great man! He who brings good things! What did you bring?
Nothing. Why do you hate us? Why? You say wetmen own
cargo. No! Blackfellas are the rich ones.

DON: Don't listen to him, Ola.

MAKIS: All the people know cargo belongs to us! How do they
know? Easy. Any man who works all day till blood runs
down sees true. Whose island is this? Who was born here?
Who works in the fields? Old man, in all your years, did you
ever see a wetman working?

PIOBA: No time.

OLA: When did you ever go to Port Moresby? When? In Port
Moresby I learnt cargo will never come to us. True?

DON: True!

OLA: So give me back my followers.

MAKIS: Port Moresby is a wetman's jungle – nothing more. What
you learn there is lies. In that good time before the wetmen
came, our ancestors gave us a rich life. True?

OLA: But that's what *I* teach.

MAKIS: No! You say wetmen's ancestors send cargo to wetmen.

OLA: Yes! It's true!

MAKIS: No! Our ancestors long to send cargo to us. They can't.
Why?

DON: Ola told you why.

MAKIS: No! Wetmen stole our ancestors!

OLA: Who told you this?

MAKIS: If there's one thing we know it's this thing: nothing
comes without good working. True?

OLA: That's true.

MAKIS: If we want good things from our ancestors we got to do a work to get it. It isn't wetmen's work that brings cargo. It's the work *we* do. We work, our ancestors should send *us* cargo. But wetmen stole them. They lie in chains! They bleed!

OLA: Oh this is true! In Port Morseby I saw our ancestors all locked up in a cage. It's true!

MAKIS: Wetmen make our ancestors send cargo just to them. We got to set them free!

(OLA *thinks about this for a moment, then he gives* DON *his book back*.)

OLA: Don, write a letter to this king. Tell him Australians stole our ancestors. He'll make them send them home.

MAKIS: You still dream of wetmen loving you.

(*He takes the portrait of the king and tears it up*.)

Break up that dream. Now, lead us!

OLA: You want me to lead your seven thousand? Why?

MAKIS: Everyone knows you. When you teach the true line everyone will follow. Let the people hear the famous native overseer say cargo will come. Lead us!

OLA: But how can we bring our ancestors home?

MAKIS: How? Fight! Fight! Fight!

DON: Wetmen have all the guns. How can we fight wetmen?

MAKIS: Guns? Who said guns? Is that the way blackfellas fight?

DON: It's how wetmen will fight us. Ola, come!

MAKIS: Guns has never been blackfellas' way. (*Indicates* PIOBA) He knows the way. Let two old roosters teach you. The first work's done already. All our villages are down. Now this is how we blackfellas bring our ancestors home.

(*He takes a vase and a tablecloth from his sack and puts them on the table. He makes passes with his hands.*

OLA, DON *and* MAMBA *watch, astonished by this.*

PIOBA *chuckles*.)

Earth soft. Sky dark. Sun dark. This island – born.

(*He takes a dead chicken from his bag, rips it open and pours its blood into the vase. Then he takes fresh, brightly coloured flowers from the sack and puts them in the vase*.)

Leaf. Bud. Green. Grew. Roots in blood water. Eye wide in black sky. We lived so long in darkness. Ola brings the sun.

(*His tone becomes conversational again.*) To make it extra
strong, a little beer. Or half a cigarette. (*He takes these from
his sack and puts them on the table. He stands proudly beside the
table.*) Ola, take your place here, next to me.
(OLA *starts to move towards the table.*)

DON: That makes cargo come? Bullshit.

PIOBA: You! This work was done long, long before the wetmen
came. Were you born in that time?

DON: No, but I can see it's rubbish. Ola, you taught us: 'Give up
cargo. Work hard.' Don't stop. Teach us how!

OLA: I always taught them, praise their ancestors, Don. True?

DON: You taught: There are no ships for blackfellas. That's all we
know is true.

MAKIS: I never tell you there are ships for blackfellas. There are
no ships for us.

OLA: No ships?

MAKIS: Our ancestors will never come in ships.

OLA: That is the only way cargo can come.

MAKIS: Did you travel to Port Moresby in a ship?

OLA: I flew.

PIOBA: True! Flew! Parrots and bees! Ha ha!

MAKIS: We clear a big, big airstrip. Wetmen can't stop
aeroplanes.

OLA: I flew!

DON: We'll have no land! Nothing! Ola!

OLA: I see it now! I see how it will come! I know this flying. Cargo
belongs to blackfellas!

MAKIS: Sun! Sinking in the sea. I, Makis, press you back into the
sky.
(*He tenses his body and exerts immense force.*
Light rises on the stage, slowly at first.)

DON: Ola!
(*Enter* SWANSI *with his eyes still bound. He gropes about, his
hands held out in front of him. He senses the presence of people.
He stops. He moves towards* PIOBA *and backs away. Towards*
MAKIS, *backs away. He moves towards* DON, *then closer. He is
about to touch* DON, *then he swings round and goes straight for*
OLA. *He clasps Ola's shoulders, then falls to his knees and clasps*

115

Ola's legs.

The light rises in a flood.)

MAKIS: You are Ola, black king of New Guinea.

(DON *runs off.*

A bird is heard singing. MAKIS *points at it.*)

First of our ancestors, broken free, flies home to welcome
you.

(*The bird sings.*

*Darkness. In the darkness bullroarers are heard, louder than
we've heard them before.*

Then a chant is taken up, soft at first but rising.

*The light comes up and a tall pole with a pumpkin on the tip
can be seen. Two strings attached to the pumpkin end in tin
cans.*

MAMBA *and* SWANSI *speak into the cans.*

The chorus is taken up by a shadowy multitude.)

MAMBA:
SWANSI:
}Ola! Ola!

CHORUS: Ola! Ola!

MAMBA:
SWANSI:
}Bring our cargo!

CHORUS: Ola! Ola!

MAMBA:
SWANSI:
}Bring us good things!

CHORUS: Ola! Ola!

MAMBA:
SWANSI:
}Bring the guns!

CHORUS: Ola! Ola!

MAMBA:
SWANSI:
}Bring the cannon!

CHORUS: Ola! Ola!

MAMBA:
SWANSI:
}Bring the jeep!

CHORUS: Ola! Ola!

MAMBA:
SWANSI:
}Start the fighting!

CHORUS: Ola! Ola!

MAMBA: ⎫
SWANSI: ⎭ Throw the wetmen.

CHORUS: Ola! Ola!

MAMBA: ⎫
SWANSI: ⎭ Into the sea!

CHORUS: Ola! Ola!

MAMBA: ⎫
SWANSI: ⎭ Drown the wetmen!

CHORUS: Ola! Ola!

MAMBA: ⎫
SWANSI: ⎭ In the sea! Cargo! Cargo! (*Etc.*)

(*The light fades.*
Darkness.
Silence.
Loud sound of the sea.)

NINE

The 'airstrip' near Bogati. Midnight. Faint moonlight. Soft lapping
of the sea.
Three tables decorated according to MAKIS *are barely visible.*
MAMBA, SWANSI *and* PIOBA *stand staring up at the sky, all in plain*
shorts and vests. For a while MAMBA *and* SWANSI *stare up in various*
directions.
PIOBA *remains still.*

MAMBA: At Yapa they got eighth ancestors home.

SWANSI: Says who?

MAMBA: I heard.

SWANSI: Eight? No time!

MAMBA: True! My brother says.

SWANSI: Your brother! He calls any shit an ancestor. One time he
said a cabbage is his ancestor just 'cause he had one there.
It's easy to reach eight that way. Easy.
(*They stare up at the sky.*
PIOBA *coughs hoarsely and sits down.*)

PIOBA: Aeroplane – this is an old, old rooster calling you. We
built a nest for you – so big. So hurry up! Come quick time.
(*Cough. Cough.*) Please, aeroplane, come soon.

117

(*He coughs again and remains seated, staring up.*)

MAMBA: They built an airstrip at Ouba too.

SWANSI: Says who?

MAMBA: I heard.

SWANSI: At Ouba?

MAMBA: My brother says. And also at Usina.

SWANSI: It will come here number one.

MAMBA: They build a nest at Bongu. Also Dein.

SWANSI: We built our airstrip first. True?

MAMBA: What does Ola say?

SWANSI: He says it's true.

(*Enter* OLA. *He wears shorts, shirt and sandals, a whistle round his neck and an elaborate head-dress similar to the one* MAKIS *wore.*)

SWANSI: Only three ancestors came so far, kiap.

OLA: How long have missionaries said Jesus Christ will come? Since I was small, small. In six days we cleared all this jungle floor.

MAMBA: So how long now, kiap?

OLA: Don't ask me how long. You got to set all our ancestors free. Make cargo come!

(*He blows his whistle.*

SWANSI, MAMBA, PIOBA: (*Singing.*)

Come down! Come down! Come down!
Aeroplane! Aeroplane!
Bzzz! Bzzz! Bzzz!
Vroom! Vroom!
We have built you a beautiful nest!
Come down!
Bzzz. Bzzz.
Vroom-ooom!

(*As they chant and repeat this spell they hold their arms out in imitation of an aeroplane and run about.*

MAMBA *and* SWANSI *sing and dance vibrantly.* PIOBA *is sick and feeble.*

OLA *watches.*

SWANSI, MAMBA *and* PIOBA *stop their dancing and take up casual positions.*)

OLA: You boys, care for Pioba. We got to keep him till his cargo comes.

(OLA *gives* PIOBA *a cigarette.* PIOBA *lights it immediately with a box of matches. He smokes and coughs.*)

Stay full of life, old man. Now sleep.

(MAMBA, SWANSI *and* PIOBA *lie down at the side. The stage grows darker.*)

Now this island sleeps. From – oh so many villages – Gumbi, Galek, Ganglau – all the people come here to Bogati. Each night my thirteen thousand followers lie around this nest to sleep. Old ladies with their heads propped on a stone. Boys sleeping in a circle by that tree. Girls curled up tight like prawns to keep them warm. Tonight where they believe in me and Makis they lie peacefully. But where they never heard my name – oh, worry, worry, where to find food, how to keep warm, hardly sleeping. Ha ha ha. Yes, here we know: soon, soon. Even fish sleep easy here. How gentle is the sea. Oh sea, in that old time these people waited for some happiness from you. But you were wild and greedy. You raise your neck, roll out your white, wet tongue and swallow up our progress.

(*Enter* JOANA. *She wears a black cloak round her shoulders.*)

Olright. We found another road. We see now who our true friend always is: this sky. Oh sky, you are the true king of the people. Always gentle, always true. You can guide us. You see everything. Ha ha. Did you see last night? The night before? The women ask, not me. Ola, let me lie with you! Headmen send me girls. I make their babies strong.

JOANA: Ola?

OLA: It's me, girl. Don't be frightened. No one's here. Do you want me?

JOANA: I came back to find you.

(*She folds her cloak around him.*)

OLA: Joana! Oh, rough seas. My heart is pounding! You're an ancestor! You've come back home.

JOANA: There are no ancestors. Death is bones and rotting in the mud. I died to bring these people cargo.

OLA: It's coming – soon.

119

JOANA: I will show you what will come.

(*The light rises quickly. We see a view of the sea from an island in the Pacific. Palm trees, atolls, turquoise sea – just as on the postcards and in the movies.*

Joana's cloak is seen to be a towel. She is dressed for the beach in fashionable Western style.)

OLA: It's come! Cargo has come!

(*Enter PIOBA in uniform (khaki shorts, khaki shirt with red piping, khaki cap with red piping). He carries a notice on a stick reading, 'Do not talk to strangers. The management takes no responsibility for valuables beyond this point.'*

Enter from the opposite side YIM, dressed in a smart and expensive suit, wearing sunglasses, with a camera slung round his neck.)

PIOBA: Do not talk to valuables! Don't steal beyond this point! Do not talk to valuables! Don't steal beyond this point!

YIM: Ola, wetmen like you. Now there will be plenty, plenty good jobs for a smart New Guinea man. They'll need leaders, ministers, advisers.

JOANA: You got cargo. Did it bring you happiness?

YIM: You bet your life! I got ten black boys working for me now. I'm finished teaching wild boys from the bush. These days I supervise. Once a month I go home to my village. I lie in a hammock in the sun. My grandpa tells me stories. How the people lived in the old times. All the rituals. All the dances.

PIOBA: You listen to that shit? What past is this he tells you was so good? When Australians made us hop, hop, hop and beat us! When English people took our homes and beat us? When Japanese killed all our headmen? Or when the Germans smashed our children's heads with clubs? Oh that was good times. Very happy. Look at me now. I got a uniform. I got some words here on my sign. When did I ever get such good, good pay?

(*Enter MAMBA and SWANSI wearing bathing costumes and sunglasses. MAMBA carries a portable radio playing loud music. They are sharing an ice cream.*)

The boss says I can't let you on this beach till after five.

You buy no drinks. You mess with customers. Hey. Boy.
Give an old man a smoke.
(SWANSI *gives him a cigarette*.)
JOANA: Do you love cargo?
(MAMBA *and* SWANSI *laugh*.)
SWANSI: Sure. We love cargo.
MAMBA: His uncle's got a night spot on the beach. Those tourist
    chicks!
SWANSI: They sure mean business.
MAMBA: You owe me seven bucks.
SWANSI: No time! You picked up more than me.
PIOBA: Get off this beach. Go on!
SWANSI: We only want to rest our feet.
MAMBA: We won't harm any wetmen.
PIOBA: So you say. No. I'll get the sack. Come after sunset.
    There's room for you then. You got a smoke?
    (SWANSI, MAMBA, PIOBA *and* YIM *wander off*.)
JOANA: You got to wake the people, Ola. It's dawn! The sea is
    white! Ola, you *got* to wake them. I got to go back to my
    mud. Don't lose your life in waiting, Ola.
OLA: No. I'm leader of my thirteen thousand. I know our
    ancestors will bring us cargo. One day soon dawn will come
    and all the people *will* wake up. They'll stand and look up
    at the sky and there we will see aeroplanes! Ancestors
    bringing cargo! The whole sky full of aeroplanes! Oh that
    day! We will not be rubbish anymore!
    (*In the distance the sound of a helicopter approaching rapidly.*
    OLA *stands amazed. He follows the path of the helicopter across
    the sky.*
    The helicopter is just above the stage and very loud.
    MAMBA *and* SWANSI *run on*.)
MAMBA: Ola! It's here!
SWANSI: It's here!
OLA: We will not work for wetmen anymore!
MAMBA: Cargo has come!
SWANSI: It's here!
OLA: We will be rich! We will be strong! We will have
    happiness!

(The helicopter lands (off-stage). The gusts of wind it causes blows the vases on the tables over.

Enter SCOVILL. *He is as amazed to see* OLA *as* OLA *is to see him.)*

SCOVILL: Sergeant Ola! You're under arrest!

(They stare at each other.

Darkness.

Silence.

Sound of the sea – waves breaking on the beach over and over.)

TEN

Five years have passed.

The beach at Bogati.

The sun is very bright – so bright that, unless wearing sunglasses, it is constantly necessary to shade one's eyes with one's hands.

The back of Gau's one-room wood house. A door. A table with cheap trade items, laid out in rows: leather belts, bottle openers, mirrors, cheap cigarette lighters, combs, penknives, etc.

On the wall of the house are a number of posters – part of Gau's election campaign. They have slogans such as 'You vote Gau – you vote him number one'. 'Vote Gau and get a special trading credit'. 'Vote Gau – he helps the people'. 'Gau stands for honesty and hard work'.

A small amount of home-made bunting has been hung out.

To one side a flag-pole flying the Australian flag. To another stand three small crates and two sacks of roots vegetables. There is another small table near the centre of the stage on which is a table-cloth and a vase of bright flowers. GAU *is sitting at this table on one of Scovill's wicker chairs (scene seven) filling out a form. He is dressed in perfect replica of* YIM *(scene five). His hat is on the table.*

GAU: Moro! Moro – come out here!

(Enter MORO *from the house, wearing a dress similar to the one she wore in scene three. She is combing her hair. In contrast to* GAU's *bustle she has an air of dejection.)*

See what's in those crates.

*(MORO *goes to the crates. She lifts the lid of one.)*

MORO: Cocoa.

122

GAU: One crate cocoa.
(*He marks it on the sheet.* MORO *moves to the next crate. She lifts the lid.*)

MORO: Coffee.

GAU: One crate coffee. How long have we done this working?

MORO: Five years.

GAU: This is the worst week that we ever had. Only two crates I can sell. No one's working. Kiap's got to make them work.

MORO: The people are too busy making votes to work.

GAU: Rubbish. The voting's done.

MORO: Who won?

GAU: We don't know yet who won. It takes kiap days and days to count up all the votes. You got to learn this paper, Moro. If I win, I got to go for the local government council every month. Then you got to do this work.

MORO: You think you'll win, Gau?

GAU: Look at this paper. (*Hiccup*) This is a cocoa here. You see?

MORO: I don't need to learn. You'll never win.

GAU: The people vote for me.

MORO: Not all the people.

GAU: I don't need all the people. (*Hiccup*) I just need half. That's all.
(*Enter* DON. *He is dressed in long trousers, white shirt and sandals. Unlike Gau's clothes, these are rather tattered.*)

DON: Well you can take down all these flashy things.

GAU: Get out! We never talk to People's Party here.

DON: Talk or don't talk. The People's Party won!

GAU: Who says you won?

DON: Everybody. So we won. That's the kind of system we got now. If the people say you won, you won.

GAU: You People's Party fellas are too angry. You suffer from a mental poisoning put in your blood by Communists.

DON: Where's kiap? I hear kiap talking. Who got good things in Bogati these days? Kiap and you. That's all.

GAU: What I got I work for. Tell him, Moro. It's work to come here every day, inspect the crates and bags, write on this paper. It's work, it's work to find someone to buy. Tell him.

MORO: (*Wearily*) Yes. It's true. It's work.

GAU: It's work! It's work!

DON: And what you got from all this working?

GAU: What I got? Soft shirt. Nice pants. Strong shoes. This hat. Tell him what you got.

MORO: I got this dress. I got a whole box of tinned meat.

DON: With People's Party on the council everyone will get the same.

SCOVILL: (*Off*) Anyone there? Gau! Gau! Where the hell is everyone?

GAU: Don't let kiap see you here. Go! Go!

(*Enter* SCOVILL. *He wears sunglasses.*)

SCOVILL: Ah there you are.

GAU: It's People's Party, kiap.

(SCOVILL *takes off his glasses, then puts them on again.*)

SCOVILL: I see. In the circumstances, perhaps you'd better stay.

(SCOVILL *sits at the table.* MORO *sits on a crate and stares off.*)

I might as well tell you both together. I've had to cancel the election.

DON: No time! This is the people's voting. Only we can cancel it.

GAU: If kiap gives us elections, he can take it back.

DON: We won! That's why. Oh there'll be fighting now.

SCOVILL: No, Don. You didn't win.

DON: So why'd you cancel it?

SCOVILL: Here is the result of the election in the Bogati ward of the local government council elections. The number of votes for Mr Don Orokolo, People's Party: one hundred and twenty-two. The number of votes for Mr Gau Rigo, Independent: one.

(GAU *and* DON *look bewildered.*)

The number of votes for Sergeant Ola was eight hundred and ninety-nine.

GAU: But Ola didn't stand in the election, kiap!

DON: Ola's in jail!

SCOVILL: For Gomuru district. People's Party candidate: forty-six. Independent candidate: seven. Sergeant Ola: nine hundred and forty-six. Ouba district. One hundred and twenty-eight. Seventeen. Seven hundred and twenty-one. I have another ten results here. Ola won them all.

GAU: You got to cancel this election, kiap.
SCOVILL: What does the People's Party say? We asked the
    people: 'Who'd you vote for?' They say: 'Ola.' What else can
    I do? So go back to your party. Tell them what's occurred.
    Press on. Gau – come inside. I want to hear what ideas
    you've got on getting people back to work.
    (SCOVILL *goes inside the house.*
    GAU *tears down the bunting and posters.*)
MORO: Don't tear them, Gau. Use them next time.
GAU: The kiap can't trust the people, see? There won't be a next
    time.
DON: There will! Trust me. There will!
    (GAU *goes inside the house.*)
    Kiap says Gau got just one vote. That must be the one he
    made. You didn't vote for Gau?
    (MORO *shakes her head.*)
    For who then? Me?
MORO: No. Ola.
DON: Why? How long has Ola promised cargo? When you people
    find your voting's wasted, you'll cry!
MORO: I cry sometimes. I been waiting for a long time too. Gau
    was always so quick to believe any new thing in his hand is
    cargo. Anything. That pants. That shirt. That hat. That isn't
    cargo. How can it be? He bought it in a shop.
DON: There is no cargo. What we get, we get by working.
MORO: Oh no. Cargo is good things without the working. Like
    wetmen do. That's what I'm waiting for.
DON: But wetmen only do no work because we work for them.
    Everything they got is ours. Unless we take it, it will never
    come.
MORO: Never?
DON: Never.
MORO: No. That I can't believe.
    (*Enter* MAMBA *and* SWANSI. *They are dressed as policemen as in
    Scene One.*)
MAMBA: Kiap!
SWANSI: Kiap!
MAMBA: Where is he?

SWANSI: Where is that damn kiap?

(SCOVILL *opens the door and looks out.*)

MAMBA: Oh there you are.

SWANSI: We got him.

SCOVILL: Well done. Bring him in.

(*Exit* MAMBA *and* SWANSI.

Enter OLA. *He wears khaki shorts and shirt and has handcuffs on.* MAMBA *and* SWANSI *follow.*)

SCOVILL: (*To* DON *and* MORO) Leave us alone. I'll give you orders later.

DON: Scovill, one time I sat in your pretty chair. It suits the People's Party well to sit there. We're going to sit there soon.

(*Exit* DON. MORO *goes into the house.*)

SCOVILL: You two, stand further off.

(MAMBA *and* SWANSI *sit some distance away.*)

OLA: You took me out of jail, kiap. Why? Is my time done?

SCOVILL: No. You've only served five years. By rights you've got two more to go.

OLA: Then take me back. I've been a good fella in jail. I don't want trouble now.

SCOVILL: What do you know about the local government elections?

OLA: About what, kiap?

SCOVILL: Do you know you've been elected by every single district on this coast.

OLA: I won them all?

(SCOVILL *eyes him a moment, then stands and undoes his handcuffs.*)

SCOVILL: What did I do to deserve you, Ola? Every time I've got a problem, you're the one who's caused it, you're the only bugger who can sort it out.

OLA: I'm a prisoner, kiap. I can't sort nothing now.

SCOVILL: I suppose you know my problem.

OLA: No one's working on plantations.

SCOVILL: Not a soul. And why?

OLA: I don't know, kiap.

SCOVILL: You know. Better than anyone else – you bloody know. Even after five long years they still live in hope – one day, one day, one day. Look Sergeant, we understand each other, true? I'll be quite frank. Gau's fine at buying and selling. But he's not got much up there. He's got no notion how to get them working. Meanwhile, the plantation bosses are after my blood. How can they run their businesses if no one works for, them?

OLA: They can't!

SCOVILL: They can't!

OLA: True!

SCOVILL: True! Will you stop that! If they stay away from work much longer, I'll lose my job.

OLA: That's bad, bad, kiap. You ought to get promotion, not the sack.

SCOVILL: Thanks heaps. Look, I've got two alternatives. Either I cancel the elections and bring the army in to force the buggers back. And that will work. Believe me. But it looks bad. As if I can't control this place.
(OLA *smiles broadly*.)
Or else I can declare you winner and let you pick a team to form a council. On one condition.

OLA: I got to get the people back to work.

SCOVILL: What do you say?

OLA: No.

SCOVILL: Why?

OLA: Can't you see, kiap? Ho ho ho. It's easy. You made me go to jail for five years. Five! I am a no good man. How can I form a council?

SCOVILL: Sit down. You must be tired. Let's talk this through again.
(OLA *sits in the wicker chair*.)
You want a cigarette? Here, take the pack.
(OLA *takes it*. SCOVILL *lights his cigarette with a cigarette lighter*.)
Seen one of these before? Good, isn't it? Let me explain this in the most straightforward terms. We're doing something new now. It's called democracy.

OLA: Democracy.

SCOVILL: That means each district has a small, small government of its own. All the people have a vote. They choose the men they want to follow. These people chose you.

OLA: What must I do?

SCOVILL: The Australian government is very far away. They don't know what you need here, do they?

OLA: That's true.

SCOVILL: But when you've got your democratic council, you can tell the Australian government what you need.

OLA: And will we get what we need?

SCOVILL: In time you will. It's just the same as us. We tell the government in England what we need.

OLA: Oh no. I know that king of England. He made me overseer. Then he let me go to jail. That king – he won't do any bloody thing we blackfellas tell him.

SCOVILL: Sergeant, can't you forget all that? The king of England's dead now, anyway.

OLA: He's dead?

SCOVILL: We've got a new leader now. A queen.

OLA: We got a queen? This council, kiap, is it a house?

SCOVILL: Oh yes, it's a big, big house with high stone walls. You know it, Ola. My old admin. building.

OLA: I know it, yes, so well!

SCOVILL: Outside the gate is one big man of stone holding a sword.

OLA: And inside?

SCOVILL: Yes. Inside –

OLA: I know what's inside.

(SCOVILL *looks at* OLA, *perturbed by the intensity of his speech*.)

SCOVILL: The local democratic government council –

OLA: Is the way we get the things the Australian government can't see that we need. True?

SCOVILL: True.

OLA: Oh Mr Scovill, how long have you known me? Since we fought side by side in that old war. So many years. I'm asking you, why didn't you tell me this line before?

SCOVILL: We've never had democracy before. You understand me now?

OLA: Oh yes, yes, yes. I do.

SCOVILL: So will you go on the council?

(OLA *stands.*)

OLA: Yes. I'll go.

SCOVILL: Well done. I'll go and declare you winner in all the
thirteen districts. I'll meet you in my office. Excellent. Press
on.

(*Exit* SCOVILL.

OLA *takes a cigarette from the pack and lights it with the lighter.*
He takes a deep draw.)

OLA: So now we got a local government council. We got a small,
small government just for us. We tell the Australian
government. The Australian government tells the Queen. A
woman will do anything we tell her. So now we got a council.
We got democracy. These beautiful new wetmen's things
will bring us what we need.

(*He walks down to the shore and looks out.*

To himself) Cargo. Cargo.

Desire

For Judith Cornell

CHARACTERS

KINDO GOREDEMA
ROSEMARY, his older daughter
SHUPI, his younger daughter
AMBUYA, his mother
GAUDENCIA KAMBADA, chairman of the village committee
DANGER, her son
WIRELESS CHIKAMBO
LENA, his wife
FREEDOM, his daughter
JERICHO ZINDOGA, a government employee

The play is set in a village in the Zambezi Valley in the far north of Zimbabwe in 1980. There is an interval between scenes six and seven.

Desire was first performed at the Almeida Theatre, London, on 10 May 1990. It was directed by Andrei Serban and designed by Richard Hudson.

AUTHOR'S NOTE
I would like to thank the committee of the George Orwell Memorial Award for a grant that financed an early stage of the writing of this play.

ONE

Before dawn.
A bridge over a stream.
ROSEMARY *waits in the darkness.*
FREEDOM *rides in on a bicycle, dismounts. She wears military*
camouflage.
FREEDOM: (*Calling softly*) Rosemary!
ROSEMARY: I'm here.
FREEDOM: You've come!
    (*She holds out the bicycle to* ROSEMARY.)
    Get on.
ROSEMARY: I've come to tell you: I can't go with you.
FREEDOM: Why? All your friends are with me in the bush.
    They're full of fight.
ROSEMARY: Don't try to pressure me!
FREEDOM: You want to be with us.
ROSEMARY: Do I?
FREEDOM: I know your heart. Let's move. This place is
    dangerous.
ROSEMARY: Who can see us?
FREEDOM: There are always spies.
ROSEMARY: I'm going home.
FREEDOM: But why?
ROSEMARY: I've got a pain.
    (*Silence.*)
FREEDOM: What kind of pain?
    (ROSEMARY *takes Freedom's hand, shows her.*)
    That's nothing.
ROSEMARY: Feel!
FREEDOM: It's fear. We're all afraid.
ROSEMARY: Of?
FREEDOM: Dying. Time passes, it's gone.
    (*Dawn appears over the mountain.*)
    The sun is rising. People will start moving in the village. (*She*
    holds out the bicycle.) Take it.

ROSEMARY: If I'm with you, who'll look after my father, wash his clothes, cook his food?

FREEDOM: Who cares? This is a war!

ROSEMARY: My mother's dead. He needs me.

FREEDOM: We all need you. To be strong! To fight!

SHUPI: (*Off*) Rosemary!

ROSEMARY: Too late.

SHUPI: (*Off*) Rosemary!

(FREEDOM *mounts the bicycle.*)

FREEDOM: I've loved you since you were so high. When it's dark look for me. I'll come for you again.

(*She rides off.*

SHUPI *runs on. She is crippled in her right leg.*)

SHUPI: Rosemary!

(AMBUYA *and* LENA *run on.*)

AMBUYA: Did you look by the river?

SHUPI: She's not there.

AMBUYA: In the fields?

SHUPI: I ran down to the gully.

AMBUYA: Try the other way.

(SHUPI *runs off.*)

LENA: Maybe she took a walk?

AMBUYA: So early? What for?

LENA: The war's over. The curfew's lifted. If people want to put one foot down then another and go on and on, no matter what the time, they can just go.

SHUPI: (*Off*) Rosemary!

LENA: You think she's run away?

(SHUPI *runs on.*)

SHUPI: She's nowhere.

AMBUYA: Where could she run?

LENA: Back to that man's bed.

SHUPI: She wouldn't do it.

LENA: It's what she did before.

AMBUYA: Poor girl. Always the same. She hasn't got a mother she can turn to. Something's wrong, she puts on her shoes, runs.

SHUPI: She could have run back to him any time. Today she'll hear the judgement of the court: is she allowed to go to him or not. What good's running away?

LENA: My daughter didn't run. They shot her. She was on her bicycle. She fell. Died. On this bridge.

(*The sun rises.*

ROSEMARY *is sprawled on the bridge. They see her. They stand astonished. After a moment,* ROSEMARY *wakes, leaps up. Silence.*)

Why are you lying here?

SHUPI: Your hair's a tangle. Look. Her dress. It's torn.

LENA: Why there? Why on the spot I found my daughter's body? A! (*She picks up a clod of earth.*) Her blood! The rain can't wash it. It's thick in the earth where you were lying. What's going on? What are you trying to do?

(KINDO *rides in on a bicycle exactly like Freedom's. He has a hoe over his shoulder. He stops.*)

(*To* KINDO) Your daughter was sleeping on the spot I found my daughter. I want to know the reason.

KINDO: Rosemary?

ROSEMARY: I couldn't sleep. I came out for fresh air. Maybe I lay down.

KINDO: Her neck is bleeding.

LENA: Bleeding?

AMBUYA: (*Going to* ROSEMARY) Where?

KINDO: (*To* AMBUYA) Mother, I told you: look after her!

(ROSEMARY *is about to faint.*)

SHUPI: (*Going to her*) Rosemary!

(KINDO *throws down his bicycle, takes* ROSEMARY *from* AMBUYA, *steadies her.*)

KINDO: OK. OK.

(*He takes off his shirt, uses it to staunch the wound on her neck.*) Keep still.

AMBUYA: It's just a scratch. Maybe she scraped it on a tree.

(LENA *throws down the clod of earth.*)

LENA: (*To* SHUPI) But this is where we found the body. Isn't it? Right here. Right on this bridge.

ROSEMARY: I'm sorry, father, if I've worried you.

KINDO: Me? Worried? About what?

137

ROSEMARY: Did you think I'd run away?

KINDO: I plant maize, weeds grow, *that* makes me worried. I know you won't leave me.

> (*He throws his shirt to* AMBUYA.)

Wash it. When it's dry bring it to me.

> (*He mounts his bicycle, starts to ride off.*)

SHUPI: Father.

> (KINDO *stops.*)

Don't forget. The court will judge Rosemary's case at ten.

KINDO: But it's the people's court. Not so? Then it must wait for the people. (*To* AMBUYA) Take her to rest. I'm going to cut my weeds.

> (*He rides off.*)

TWO

Mid-morning. A clearing under a tree in the centre of the village.
GAUDENCIA, *chairman of the village committee, sits on a wooden chair, sewing.* SHUPI *sits near her. She takes the minutes of the court proceedings.*

ROSEMARY *and* AMBUYA *sit together as do* LENA *and her husband* WIRELESS.

Rosemary's husband JERICHO *sits to one side.* KINDO *sits on the other.*

Apart from JERICHO *and* ROSEMARY, *everyone's clothes are in tatters. Rosemary's dress is old but whole.* JERICHO *wears a smart khaki uniform and holds a metal spray gun.*

GAUDENCIA *raises her right fist.*

GAUDENCIA: Forward with the new committee!

> (*Everyone raises their right fists.*)

ALL: Forward!

GAUDENCIA: Forward with the year of reconciliation!

ALL: Forward!

GAUDENCIA: Down with treachery and lies!

ALL: Down with them!

GAUDENCIA: Forward with democracy!

ALL: Forward!

GAUDENCIA: Good. Before we begin. I know you all feel deeply

about what we're going to hear. But everyone in this valley is
hungry. Since sunrise we've been in our fields. We need to rest
before the sun gets cool and we can work again. So, comrades,
do your level best to keep your speeches brief. Good. Number
two. People keep asking me: during the war no one could
farm, our government promised till the harvest comes they'd
send us rations, where are they? I'm chairman of this village.
Yesterday I caught the bus. I went up the mountain to the
District Office. I asked those young men: 'Where are our
rations?' They said: 'You're not forgotten. Sign this docket.
Trust us. Your food will come.'

(JERICHO *takes off his jacket.*

GAUDENCIA *finishes what she is sewing.*)

LENA: (*To* WIRELESS) How does she look to you?

WIRELESS: Worn out. Like you, like me.

LENA: If you'd seen her on the bridge.

WIRELESS: I'll watch her, hear what she says, then I'll try to work
out what it means.

(SHUPI *takes off her blouse – she wears a vest beneath – and holds
it out to* GAUDENCIA, *who holds out a length of thread.*)

GAUDENCIA: That's all that's left.

SHUPI: Try at least.

GAUDENCIA: My dear, I can't work miracles.

SHUPI: Uh uh. I know you.

(GAUDENCIA *takes the blouse, starts sewing.*)

GAUDENCIA: Comrade Jericho, you brought this case. I hand over
to you.

JERICHO: Forward with democracy!

ALL: Forward!

JERICHO: OK. I don't know where to start.

GAUDENCIA: At the beginning.

JERICHO: OK. I was born with a smile on my face. All my life I've
been quite free and easy. But this business with Rosemary . . .
OK, I'll keep it brief. Rosemary is my wife. She's lived with
me a mile along the road, there at the flygate where I work, one
year. One day she said she wants to see her grandmother, her
sister and so on. She came here. Now she wants to come home.
There's an obstacle. Her father. He says no.

139

GAUDENCIA: Comrade Kindo, I hand over to you.

KINDO: A! A! A! Look! I thought the ground was dry. It's wet. My pants are wet. Shupi, go home. Bring me another pair.

SHUPI: You haven't got another pair.

KINDO: I mean my trousers. You can't mean I haven't got even one other pair? Well, go home anyway. I'm hungry. Cook me some eggs and meat.

SHUPI: We've got no food.

KINDO: A! A! A! No food. He's got a uniform, a government job, they give him food, a house, a salary. What have I got? The fact is, it's her choice. She wants to be with me.

JERICHO: You force her!

KINDO: How? Are there chains on her feet?

JERICHO: This is a court of law. Am I right?

GAUDENCIA: You're right.

JERICHO: Let's look at law. I paid brideprice for her.

GAUDENCIA: You did?

JERICHO: One hundred and twenty-seven dollars.

GAUDENCIA: (*To* SHUPI) Write it down.

JERICHO: One hundred and twenty-seven dollars. That's what he was paid. But what matters is I love her, she loves me.

KINDO: (*To* ROSEMARY) Tell them why you came here.
(*Silence.*)

JERICHO: The point is she's got some kind of pain.

GAUDENCIA: Then why not go to the clinic?

WIRELESS: Excuse me, chairman. What I want to know is, what kind of pain is this? Maybe it's the kind they can cure at the clinic, maybe not.

JERICHO: We went to the clinic.

GAUDENCIA: What did they say? Rosemary? Ignore these people. Think of me as though I were your mother. Talk only to me.

ROSEMARY: They gave me pills. I went back. Three injections. I was still suffering. My grandmother knows about roots and leaves.

AMBUYA: (*Laughs*) That's true. I do.

ROSEMARY: So I came home.

WIRELESS: Did she help you?

ROSEMARY: She did.

AMBUYA: (*Laughs*) That's true.

WIRELESS: Thank you. That's what I want to know.

JERICHO: She got well. A month went by. Another. 'My one and only joy, come home, I'm missing you.' I went to find her father there, there, there, far, far hoeing his field. 'You want her? Finish paying.' 'Are you mad? I've paid!' 'There's sixty more to come.' Another sixty dollars!

GAUDENCIA: (*To* SHUPI) Write the numbers down. (*To* JERICHO) So did you pay?

JERICHO: Love makes a man a fool.

GAUDENCIA: And did she go?

JERICHO: You can see she's here! See what I mean?

(ROSEMARY *grimaces with pain.*)

And then, you see what happens? She got sick again.

KINDO: (*To* ROSEMARY) Look at me.

(*She looks at him. He pulls a comical face. She smiles.*)

She's feeling better. My face is all the medicine she needs.

JERICHO: I'm a stranger in this place. My home is on the mountain. But I want to trust this court. The policy of our government is: any man wherever he may go must get fair play. Is it fair I should pay and she stays in his house and weeds his field?

SHUPI: Do you want someone to weed or do you want Rosemary?

JERICHO: I want justice. (*To* GAUDENCIA) They voted for you. It's your job to give justice to me.

(ROSEMARY, *in pain, tries to speak.*

WIRELESS *goes to her.*)

JERICHO: I want her home!

WIRELESS: Stop the court! She's in pain.

JERICHO: No! It's a trick. You're all plotting against me.

KINDO: OK, he paid. Yes, OK, he did. But that was not for marriage. It's a fine.

JERICHO: For what?

KINDO: Seduction of a virgin.

JERICHO: My god!

GAUDENCIA: (*To* SHUPI) Write!

JERICHO: Blue lies!

KINDO: It's true! One night war came to this village. I was

141

headman. Eight guerrillas came to talk to me. Other headmen ran straight to the whites and made reports. I supported independence. I pledged my life to help the struggle. And my daughters helped me. Shupi went with the guerrillas to the bush. She learnt to fight. Rosemary stayed here to organize supplies. (*Indicates* JERICHO) Everyone knows he was a sell-out. He lived there at the flygate with the white police.

JERICHO: Tell me, did I invent the tsetse fly? Was it my idea that if a tsetse bites a cow that cow will bite the dust? It's my job to spray every car (*He sprays*), bus (*Sprays*), truck (*Sprays*) that goes up and down the mountain to kill tsetses, to stop the spread of their sleeping disease.

KINDO: We ate bark. We slept on stones. He ate meat and rice and cuddled in clean sheets.

JERICHO: Because there was a war, should I run from my job? No. I took chemicals from whoever had them, black or white. I did my job. That is what my conscience asked of me.

KINDO: I was on a mission. He came armed to my house, forced her to go with him.

JERICHO: The truth is I found her lying on the mountain, frightened, starving, her clothes soaking wet. She'd run away from here. I didn't ask why. I gave her food, warm blankets, a place to sleep. Who could dream we'd fall in love? We did.

GAUDENCIA: (*To* ROSEMARY) Did he force you or did you run to him?

WIRELESS: No one will blame you if you tell the truth.

ROSEMARY: Father, you've very kind. But so is he. You love me, I know you do. But so does he. You miss me when I'm not with you but there's your other daughter. He's only got one wife. The war was bad. I was afraid. I ran. He found me.

GAUDENCIA: So do you want to stay or go?

(ROSEMARY *looks at* KINDO, *then goes to stand with* JERICHO.)

JERICHO: Forward with the year of reconciliation! Forward with democracy!

GAUDENCIA: (*To* SHUPI) Write. They love each other. He paid for her. (*To* JERICHO) Take her. (*To* ROSEMARY) Go with him.

JERICHO: Forward with the new committee! Thank you.

(*He puts on his jacket.* ROSEMARY *goes. He follows.*

GAUDENCIA *gives* SHUPI *her blouse.*)
GAUDENCIA: That's the best I can do.

THREE

Evening, a week later.
Jericho's yard.
ROSEMARY *is cooking over a fire.*
JERICHO, *wearing his uniform, sits playing with his spray gun,*
watching ROSEMARY *in silence.*
ROSEMARY *sweeps the yard, then goes back to cooking again.*
JERICHO: Three months ago, each day twenty, thirty, jeeps and
    trucks went up and down this road. These days? A
    wheelbarrow (*He sprays*), a donkey (*He sprays*), a cart (*He*
    sprays). What goes by? My life. I long to take you home. I
    must stay here beneath their stars, their skies. They mean
    nothing to me. I love to watch you working. You sweeping
    my yard, you cooking my food. (*Silence.*) Talk to me.
    (*Silence.*
    He throws the spray gun down.)
    Don't do that!
ROSEMARY: I'm cooking.
JERICHO: You make believe you're somewhere else. It drives me
    crazy. Where do you think you are? On your moon?
ROSEMARY: I'm here.
JERICHO: No. I can't live this way. I've got a good heart. What I
    love is talking, drinking, having a good time.
    (*He looks at her, then goes to her, puts a hand on her. She pulls*
    away.)
ROSEMARY: There's people on the road.
JERICHO: No one can see us.
ROSEMARY: There are always spies.
JERICHO: Let's go inside.
ROSEMARY: So you don't want food?
JERICHO: I want it. And I want you. And I want peace. And I
    want you to be peaceful. And I want you to be peaceful
    peacefully.
    (*She goes on cooking. He moves away from her.*)

143

So one more night I'm going to sleep alone. Oh god, give me
a transfer out of here. I'm young. This valley is a pit of
witches, liars, thieves.
(*He sits, plays with his spray can.*)
A bread van (*he sprays*), a bicycle. (*He sprays.*
ROSEMARY *brings him a plate of food.*)
Do you want to get rid of me? This doesn't just kill flies. It
wipes out dogs, cats, drivers, passers by. (*He sprays, coughs.*)
Where's my strong soap?
(*She brings him a bowl of water and soap. He washes his hands,
then smells them.*)
I stink of death. Feed me.
(*She feeds him with a spoon.*)
You're losing weight.

ROSEMARY: No.

JERICHO: I can feel. You were like a sow. Now you're a young
pig.
(*He takes the spoon, tries to feed her.*)
Put this in you.
(*She pulls away. He grabs her, holds her tight. She struggles to
get away.*)
Open up.

ROSEMARY: I ate while I was cooking.

JERICHO: Liar! Don't fight with me. Why must you always fight?
I want you to be strong and happy. Open your mouth, my
apple.
(*She breaks away from him, looks out.*)

ROSEMARY: Shupi! Shupi!
(SHUPI *runs in.*)
I've told you, it's not good for you to run.

SHUPI: I'm in a hurry.

ROSEMARY: Your leg needs rest.

SHUPI: You're wrong. It's only when I'm still this one shoots this
way, this one that. If I run I'm on wheels.

ROSEMARY: It doesn't hurt?

SHUPI: Only here, where the bullet went in. The bone is strong.
And if it does? I've got a job to do, I'm late. So it hurts me,
so?

144

ROSEMARY: Where are you going?

SHUPI: A meeting of the youth. We've had a message from headquarters. We must elect a leader.

JERICHO: What for?

SHUPI: There's work for us. (*To* ROSEMARY.) Why don't you come?

ROSEMARY: Me? Do you want me to?

JERICHO: Her? Youth? (*He laughs.*) She's a married woman. What work is this?

SHUPI: To organize the people.

JERICHO: Organize? No. These people? They go their own way. Organize but if they change their minds, want something else, that's it, end of story, bash your head on a wall.

SHUPI: But you've organized what you want.

JERICHO: In a way.

SHUPI: Me too.

> (*She runs off.*
>
> JERICHO *has been feeding himself.* ROSEMARY *takes his empty plate from him.*)

JERICHO: I wish you were a water melon. I would eat you skin and flesh and seeds.

> (ROSEMARY *puts his plate by the fire, starts to go out.*)
>
> Where are you going?

ROSEMARY: If I don't fetch firewood, you'll beat me.

JERICHO: Beat you? Me? When did I even raise my hand? Beat you? Fetch firewood, fetch anything, just go. Just go! No! Come here. If you hate me – I was a fool, I begged you, come back home – but if you hate me, why did you agree?

ROSEMARY: To be with my husband.

JERICHO: I see. Is that someone I know?

ROSEMARY: The court didn't force me. I chose to be with you.

JERICHO: The court can't order you to love. Love is fire. Yours has burnt away. I'm hot. Let me cover you just once, you'll burst into flame. Tell me you want to.

ROSEMARY: I want to.

JERICHO: Every night I'm up there on my bed, you're on the floor. Tell me you'll get in my bed.

ROSEMARY: I'll get in your bed.

145

JERICHO: But do you want to? Honestly? Tell me you do.

ROSEMARY: I do.

JERICHO: Through the whole war I wished harm to no one. I wouldn't hurt a fly if my conscience didn't tell me: do your job. But you!

GAUDENCIA: (*Off*) E – oi!

ROSEMARY: E – oi!

(GAUDENCIA *comes on carrying a basket and her shoes*.)

GAUDENCIA: How did you spend the day?

ROSEMARY: Good, if you did.

GAUDENCIA: I did.

ROSEMARY: Very good. You look worn out. Come, sit.

(GAUDENCIA *sits, rubs her feet*.)

Are you hungry? We've got plenty to eat.

(*She gives her the bowl of water, fetches her food*. GAUDENCIA *washes her hands*.)

GAUDENCIA: My dear, you make me feel I've got a home. Is no one else going to eat?

(*She soaks her feet in the bowl*.)

That's better.

(*She eats*.)

ROSEMARY: Where've you come from?

GAUDENCIA: My old home near the border. I've come footing, footing the whole way.

JERICHO: You didn't catch a bus?

GAUDENCIA: I did. But half-way the driver was so drunk that fat conductor – you know him? –

JERICHO: I know him.

GAUDENCIA: He grabbed the driver's key. He said: 'Not one yard more.' They had to wait for him to sober up. But me, my blood was running. I must move. This heel broke. (*Indicates one of her shoes*.) Maybe you've got some string?

(ROSEMARY *looks in a box*.)

You see, I heard the boys who went to fight are now on their way home. My son is one.

ROSEMARY: No string. Glue.

(*She gives a tube of glue to* GAUDENCIA *who mends the heel of her shoe*.)

146

GAUDENCIA: He knows we who lived there near the border were moved out by the soldiers. He doesn't know where to. I went to leave a message in case he goes there. But there's no village.

JERICHO: Nothing at all?

GAUDENCIA: They burnt it. Then grass and rain did their work. No, nothing, just the round earth floors.

ROSEMARY: How will he find you? What's his name?

GAUDENCIA: Herbert. He'll find me. Then I'll be the lucky one. It won't just be you.

ROSEMARY: Am I so lucky?

GAUDENCIA: Of course you are. You've got water in your taps, electricity. And food.

ROSEMARY: Did you eat enough? This pumpkin will go off. And these potatoes.
(*She puts them in Gaudencia's basket.*)
Tell me about him.

GAUDENCIA: Herbert?

ROSEMARY: Do you miss him?

GAUDENCIA: How can I answer you? Painfully. On the other hand he was fighting for my rights. Because of that he's always been with me.

ROSEMARY: Did he write letters?

GAUDENCIA: His enemies gave him no time.

JERICHO: I make a point of writing to my mother once every two years. If I'm busy or not, once every two years I drop everything.

ROSEMARY: How long has he been gone?

GAUDENCIA: He left when he was sixteen. Thirteen years.

JERICHO: You think you'll recognize him? I don't think so.

GAUDENCIA: He can come back with a thousand other boys, blind my eyes, I'll walk straight to him.
(*She puts on her shoes.*)
There, my friends, like new.

ROSEMARY: Don't go.

GAUDENCIA: When I think about my son my blood runs. I must move. Thanks for the food. Stay strong.
(*She goes.*

After a moment ROSEMARY *starts to wash the pots and dishes in silence.*)

JERICHO: It seems you've got something to give to everyone but me.

(*Silence. Then she goes to him.*)

ROSEMARY: I'm here.

JERICHO: Are you?

(*He embraces her.*)

Oh, I want to sing. Nothing must ever come between us. Nothing. Come, lie with me.

(*He lays her on a mat, puts a hand under her clothes.*)

Oh, skin and flesh and seeds.

(*After a moment:*) What? What is it?

ROSEMARY: Nothing.

JERICHO: You're crying. Why?

ROSEMARY: The pain.

JERICHO: Where?

(*She takes his hand, shows him. He pulls her clothes open.*)

Who did this?

ROSEMARY: No one.

JERICHO: Tell me! Who fought with you?

ROSEMARY: With me?

JERICHO: Bruises. Scratches. I want the truth. More! Red as blood. You're bleeding.

(ROSEMARY *breaks away from him.*)

ROSEMARY: Don't touch me! Don't touch me!

FOUR

Night.

Ambuya's yard.

AMBUYA *is sitting with* LENA *and* WIRELESS.

AMBUYA: Death is always bitter. I'm old. I've suffered. Why should I want to live? But when they cover me with earth, even my heart will cry. The earth is full of murdered children. At night I hear them. Even by day, if I'm in the field, I open my mouth, I can't sing.

LENA: Our daughter was so young. She hadn't had even one child.

WIRELESS: Not even one.

LENA: That's why she wants to come home.

AMBUYA: Yes. But to who?

(Silence.)

WIRELESS: Everyone is hungry. Many girls are sick.

LENA: You didn't see her. She was lying on the spot! There was blood on the earth. What else can it mean?

WIRELESS: Unless you know which way to look at it, it can mean anything.

LENA: So you don't want to talk to Tandiwe?

AMBUYA: Was that her name?

WIRELESS: That was what we called her. It was only when she went to fight she took another name. Others were called Scorpion, Bazooka, Terror. They called her Freedom. (To LENA) Talk to her? I want to.

AMBUYA: To kill a girl before she's given birth. They're cruel, they're very cruel.

(She gets up, looks up at the sky.)

Rain?

(LENA and WIRELESS look at the sky.)

WIRELESS: I don't think so.

AMBUYA: You'll need money to pay drummers, to buy beer. My hut was burnt and all my things. You'll need to buy new cloths, black and white.

LENA: Her husband has money. If it's her, he'll pay.

(AMBUYA sees something moving.)

AMBUYA: Go in.

(WIRELESS and LENA go into the hut.

ROSEMARY runs on, throws herself at Ambuya's feet, pulls open her clothes.)

ROSEMARY: Look at me!

AMBUYA: Who did this? You don't know?

ROSEMARY: Do you?

AMBUYA: Come to the light.

(She takes ROSEMARY into the light, examines her, then takes tubs of ointments from a basket. As she oils ROSEMARY's body, she sings to her. Then:)

Now?

149

ROSEMARY: I feel cool.

AMBUYA: And the pain?

(*She goes on oiling her.*)

ROSEMARY: Sometimes it's here, or here. Sometimes I'm well, I'm even smiling, it's still somewhere.

AMBUYA: And your husband? Does he want to sleep with you?

ROSEMARY: I want to sleep with him. I used to lie on his white sheets, all those pillows, read his magazines. It was the best time of my life.

AMBUYA: That time is gone. The dead are very jealous. After all, you can't have more than one person in you. (*She laughs. ROSEMARY leaps up.*)

ROSEMARY: You think it is?

AMBUYA: Could be. Come here. Poor girl. You always want to run.

ROSEMARY: Don't tell anybody. Please!

AMBUYA: Why? If there's one in you, you'll be so peaceful. He'll have no wars to fight, no plates to wash, no yard to sweep. I know. (*She laughs*) I've got one in me.

(LENA *and* WIRELESS *emerge.*)

ROSEMARY: Have you told them?

AMBUYA: What can they learn from me? They know you and their daughter were so close. Bread and butter, tea and sugar. She had many friends. It's you she wants.

ROSEMARY: Who wants me?

LENA: Freedom.

ROSEMARY: Freedom's dead!

WIRELESS: Yes. But she doesn't want to be.

LENA: She also wants to wear new clothes, eat food, lie with her husband.

AMBUYA: (*To* LENA) Sh! (*To* ROSEMARY) Remember? You were small. The bush. The well. You and her used to climb trees. She's there. Now. Longing for you. Suffering.

(LENA *goes to* ROSEMARY, *pulls her clothes open, looks at her.*)

LENA: Don't fight her! She can kill you! Let her come!

ROSEMARY: I can't!

WIRELESS: Only you can.

ROSEMARY: She doesn't want me. My pain has gone. That's what

I came to say. It's gone! There's nothing wrong with me.
(*She runs out.*
Silence.
AMBUYA *looks at the sky.*)
AMBUYA: Rain?
(LENA *looks at the sky.*
Rain falls heavily.)

FIVE

Afternoon, a week later.
Wireless's yard.
LENA *is cooking.*
KINDO *wheels on his bicycle. Strapped to the back is a box of bottled beer. He and* WIRELESS *are drinking.* KINDO *hands* WIRELESS *the box and lays the bicycle down.*
KINDO: Who's going to be the chairman?
WIRELESS: I propose you.
KINDO: Seconded.
WIRELESS: You propose me.
KINDO: As what?
WIRELESS: Secretary.
KINDO: You can't write.
WIRELESS: It's a drinking committee. There's no need to talk. So I've no need to write down anything.
KINDO: Good! Forward with inebriation!
WIRELESS: Forward!
KINDO: Forward with intoxication!
WIRELESS: Forward!
(*They drink.*
To LENA) What's to eat?
LENA: Wild mushrooms, wild okra.
(KINDO *gives her a bottle.*)
WIRELESS: Very good with beer.
LENA: You don't want food?
WIRELESS: We're drinking. Why eat?
LENA: Bottled beer? What good is it? You can drink and die.
KINDO: Rosemary is better. No more aches and pains. Her

151

husband's happy. He sent money to me. What must I do? Just sit and feel grateful? To him? I won't. I'll drink it away. (*He drinks. Indicates* WIRELESS.) I asked him what he wanted. (*He takes lengths of black and white cloth from the box*.) And needle. And thread.

(*He gives these things to* WIRELESS.)

Someone's going to dance. He won't say who.

(LENA *takes the cloth, needle and thread, sits and starts to sew the two pieces together lengthwise.*

WIRELESS *sits and drinks*.)

You see? I'm like the sun. I'm somewhere else, you think you don't need me. In your darkest hour I pop up again.

(SHUPI *runs on*.)

Yes? You're always hanging round. What now?

SHUPI: I'm coming from a meeting, father. I'm just passing through.

KINDO: Why don't you greet your sister?

SHUPI: Where is she?

KINDO: (*Holding up a bottle*) Here! (*He drinks, then speaks in falsetto*) Hullo everyone. My name is Rosemary. (*He laughs, drinks, own voice*) Oh what daughters I've got. One sick, one a cripple, leg like a chicken bone. (*Falsetto*) Hullo everyone. My name is Rosemary.

(SHUPI *starts to go*.)

Hey! If you're going why not take my bike?

SHUPI: Father, please.

(*She moves on*.)

KINDO: You didn't hear me? I said take my bike. Can't you see I'm drunk? Don't quarrel with me.

(SHUPI *picks up the bike*.)

Jump on it and go!

(SHUPI *tries to mount the bike, falls.*

LENA *leaps up.*

KINDO *laughs*.)

SHUPI: I don't know why you're so harsh with me.

(*She runs out*.)

LENA: It was on that bike my daughter died. When she fell, my heart stood still.

(KINDO *picks up the bike, dusts it down.*)

KINDO: I bought it the day my father died and I became the
    headman of this village. My people saw her gliding down the
    hill: 'A! It's the headman. If we've done something wrong
    we'll get hot hell.' Four, five times the handle-bars broke. I
    fixed them. The chain snapped. I learnt how to rivet. Wheels
    buckled. I got a crowbar, bent them straight. Over the years
    I screwed on five new seats. So the guerrillas asked me: 'Can
    I borrow your bike?' 'Of course, if you need it. I support the
    struggle. I'll give you everything.' Look how I got her back.
    Rusted. Brakes gone. Bumpers missing. Twisted. Bent. So,
    now we've got committees. I'm not the headman any longer.
    Who needs it. Throw away the beast.
    (*He lets the bicycle fall and drinks.*)

DANGER: (*Off*) E – oi!

WIRELESS: E – oi!
    (DANGER *comes on. He wears military camouflage, carries a
    shoulder bag.*)

DANGER: Friends, you don't know me. I'm passing through this
    valley. In a week I'm back again. I saw you from the road
    and came to ask: can I borrow your bike?
    (*Silence.*)
    OK, I'll hire it. How much do you want for, let's say, seven
    days?
    (KINDO *picks up a bit of earth, holds some out to* DANGER.)

KINDO: Eat.

DANGER: What's that?

KINDO: A bomb damaged your ears? I told you: eat!

DANGER: Is this a joke?

KINDO: Not if you want my bike.
    (DANGER *takes a bit of earth, licks it.*)

KINDO: How does it taste?

DANGER: Like shit.
    (KINDO *eats the rest of it.*)

KINDO: It's honey to me. That proves you're not from here.

DANGER: You could have asked. I would have said. What kind of
    man are you?

KINDO: That's what *I* want to know.

DANGER: In the war I was called Danger. I'm from this valley but not from here.

KINDO: From where? This side or that?

DANGER: From over there.

KINDO: Then you can't take my bike. (*He laughs.*) I never liked those people who live there.

DANGER: My! Ten years of struggle and we're still divided? This side of the valley, that side. Has nothing changed?

KINDO: You comrades buggered up my bike. I won't lend it again.

DANGER: (*To* LENA) I've walked far. It seems I've got to walk again. Can you spare something to eat?

KINDO: There's no food.

DANGER: None at all?

KINDO: Scratch in the bush. Pick your own roots and weeds.

WIRELESS: It's true. We've got nothing. We're still waiting for our rations to come.

DANGER: Oh ho! Now I know where I am. (*He laughs*) Goodness. My my my.

KINDO: What are you laughing for?

DANGER: Oh, bad news, bad news. Do you want to hear? Before I walked down the mountain, I took a breather at the District Office. They were almost dead from laughing. Shall I tell you why? Village chairmen from all over go there, make demands for food, get it next day. Your chairman is so shy! She sits on the grass in the back yard, gets out some knitting, never says a word. One day a comrade went to ask, what does she want? She hardly looked at him. 'Nothing. Please don't let me waste your time.' An hour passes. She folds up her knitting, walks down to the bus, goes home again. Oh my, they're laughing there. But then they stop laughing and wonder: what kind of men are you? We gave our blood so you could vote. You vote for her, you throw our blood away.
(KINDO *picks up his bicycle, tries to mount it, can't manage it, holds it out to* DANGER.)

KINDO: Take it. Ride to the District Office. Tell them, me, Kindo, I was headman. I'm coming now to get food for my people.

154

DANGER: Me ride up there? For you? But I'm from that side of the valley. (*He picks up his bag.*) I left my people thirteen years ago. I'm going to find them. Comrades, stay strong.
(*He goes.*)

KINDO: Forward with democracy! The chairman lied! Throw her chair over! Someone else goes in! I'll do it! Forward with the new committee!
(*He tries to mount the bicycle, fails, throws it down.*)
I'm too old for this game.
(*He sits.*)
Tell me why I'm thinking of my wife. She could take a bag of maize seeds, sow an acre in an afternoon. She knew every kind of fertilizer, how to mix them, how much to use. She could cook a goat (*Snaps his fingers*), and it was done. Maybe I'm just hungry. Maybe.
(*LENA is still sewing,* WIRELESS *drinks.*)

GAUDENCIA: (*Off*) E – oi!

LENA: E – oi!
(GAUDENCIA *enters.* ROSEMARY *follows carrying a sack of vegetables.* GAUDENCIA *is knitting as she walks.*)

GAUDENCIA: You're here?

LENA: I'm here.

GAUDENCIA: Look what I've got. Onions, potatoes, turnips. I'm just one. Let me share them with you.
(*She takes the bag, opens it.*)

LENA: A! A! You've saved our lives.
(*She claps and ululates to* GAUDENCIA.)

GAUDENCIA (*Of* ROSEMARY) Thank her. She gave them to me.
(LENA *looks at* ROSEMARY.)
She's got so strong. She carried the whole bag from the flygate.
(LENA *takes onions and potatoes from the sack.*)
And she gave me this wool.

KINDO: Still knitting.

GAUDENCIA: It's a scarf. Do you like the shade?

KINDO: For who?

GAUDENCIA: My son.

KINDO: Your son? Rosemary, I'm glad to see you. Come sit here, talk to me.

(ROSEMARY *goes to* KINDO.)
You've got nothing to say? You want to drink?
(*He opens a bottle for her. She shakes her head.*)
You'll take nothing from me?

ROSEMARY: It makes me ill.

KINDO: Your husband said you were better.

ROSEMARY: I am.

KINDO: So, chairman, your son. He's coming home, is he?

GAUDENCIA: All the boys who went to fight are on their way.

KINDO: They've come already. Months ago.

GAUDENCIA: Not all. Herbert will be here soon. (*Of her knitting*) I want this done by then.

KINDO: I see. And our rations?

GAUDENCIA: Any day.

KINDO: Your Herbert, which side did he fight on?

ROSEMARY: Father, let's go look at your field. I want to see how high the maize is. Come, I'll help you weed.

KINDO: (*To* GAUDENCIA) Did you see his uniform? Did you? Many boys come home. 'Where have you been?' 'We ran to join the comrades.' Rubbish. They just ran.

GAUDENCIA: My son told me: 'Mother.' 'Yes?' 'I have to go and fight.' To take a knife and cut would hurt him less than to ask for who. Where's Shupi? I've got piles of paper work. She can give me a hand.

KINDO: If a boy is not back yet, he won't come.

ROSEMARY: Father!

GAUDENCIA: No, no.

KINDO: Like our rations, that boy's gone for good.

GAUDENCIA: I know he will.

KINDO: How do you know?

GAUDENCIA: I heard him in the wind.

KINDO: The wind? (*He laughs.*)

GAUDENCIA: 'Mother,' he said, 'Don't give up. Wait for me.'

KINDO: So that's how they did it.

GAUDENCIA: Did what?

ROSEMARY: Chairman, I'll help you with your papers. Let's go.

KINDO: They took him in a helicopter, tied a rope around his neck, kicked him out into thin air, let him swing. That was

156

the cry you heard.
GAUDENCIA: Herbert will come!
  (*Without anyone noticing,* ROSEMARY *goes.*)
KINDO: Where are our rations?
GAUDENCIA: I went to see them on the mountain. I signed the
  docket. They promised me.
  (*Silence as everyone looks at her.*)
KINDO: Nothing will come. Nothing.
  (*He takes onions and potatoes from the sack and throws them into
  the air.*)
  Bombs were falling! Hand grenades! Watch them go! I lost
  my wife, my job as headman, my bike, Rosemary. Who says
  the war is over? It's burning inside me.
  (LENA *has finished sewing the black and white cloth.*)
LENA: It's done.
  (*She puts it over her head.*)
SHUPI: (*Off*) Rosemary!
WIRELESS: Freedom.
SHUPI: (*Off*) Rosemary!
WIRELESS: She's calling Rosemary.
  (SHUPI *runs on.*)
SHUPI: What's going on? I saw Rosemary running away.
  (*They look round. She's gone.*
  KINDO *gets on his bicycle.*)
KINDO: Where did she go?
SHUPI: Into the bush.
  (*He rides off.*)
WIRELESS: Help me find her.
  (*He runs off. The others follow.*)
ALL: Rosemary! Rosemary! Rosemary!

SIX

A clearing by a well.
FREEDOM *wears military camouflage. Her bicycle lies on the ground.*
ROSEMARY: I went to look at you. You were lying on the bridge.
  Your blood ran into the river. Your arms and legs were

broken, twisted round the bike. I couldn't look. I ran. I didn't stop till I was on the mountain.

FREEDOM: What can I tell you? I have to stay in shadow. Heat's a problem, more so than in life. I want to dive into the river, drink, get cool. I can't. If it rains the grass makes my feet itch, I don't know why. I only have one feeling.

ROSEMARY: Tell me.

FREEDOM: Desire.

ROSEMARY: For what?

FREEDOM: The life I could have led. And for revenge.

ROSEMARY: On who?

(*Silence.*)

FREEDOM: Your father's coming.

ROSEMARY: Here? You better go.

FREEDOM: He can't see me. I'll sit here by the well.

ROSEMARY: Just let me talk to him, explain why I'm going, then I'll come.

FREEDOM: That's what you said last time! 'Just let me tell my father.' We waited. Did you come?

ROSEMARY: They keep on asking, 'Do you want to live like this or that? With this one or with that one?' No! The answer's no! I'm here now in the bush. I won't go home. I only feel at peace when I'm with you.

(KINDO *rides on, dismounts.*)

How did you find me?

KINDO: (*He laughs*) The others ran, one there, one here. In my mind I saw two little girls. The tree, the well. Where else could you be?

(*He sits.*)

Ah, this grass is soft. The sun is warm.

ROSEMARY: You're not angry?

KINDO: I peddled for a while watching the sky. Wide. Empty. I turned on to a path. Trees, shrubs, animals. In the whole world there's no one left who wants to use me or to kill me. It's so still. I can hear thorns growing. Leaves. So here we are. Tell me. Why did you run away?

(*Silence.*)

I'm thirsty.

(ROSEMARY *goes to the well, brings him water in her hands. He drinks*.)

It's sweet. Water from you is always sweet. My father's father came out of this earth. This water is my blood, these rocks my bones. But that's over and done. I try to hold on, hold on to what's dead and gone. Maybe that's what's wrong. (*He lies on the ground*.)

Rosemary, don't leave me.

(FREEDOM *mounts her bicycle, rides round and round, then stops*.)

You love him so much?

ROSEMARY: Who?

(*Silence*.)

FREEDOM: Come.

ROSEMARY: I can't choose between you.

FREEDOM: Come!

ROSEMARY: I don't want to die.

FREEDOM: I don't want you for death. This is for struggle. I have to struggle to come here. I need your strength.

(*She picks up Kindo's bicycle and holds it out to* ROSEMARY.)

All your friends are with me. They're full of fight. Let's move. This place is dangerous.

ROSEMARY: Who can see us?

FREEDOM: There are always spies.

(ROSEMARY *takes the bicycle, mounts it*.)

That's it! You want to. Oh, you want to.

(ROSEMARY *is riding Kindo's bicycle*. FREEDOM *mounts her own. They start to ride round and round each other*.)

VOICES: (*Off*) Rosemary! Rosemary!

(FREEDOM *rides off*.

ROSEMARY *goes on riding round*.

WIRELESS, SHUPI, LENA *and* GAUDENCIA *run on*.

KINDO *leaps up, watches*.)

ROSEMARY: Forward with the struggle of the people! Down with racism and exploitation!

WIRELESS: It's her! She's come!

ROSEMARY: Forward with the struggle of the people! Down with racism and exploitation!

159

WIRELESS: We'll brew beer! We'll play the drums! You've come!
Freedom, you've come!

SEVEN

Night, two weeks later. Wireless's yard.
To one side stands a large metal drum full of beer.
From nearby comes the sound of drumming.
GAUDENCIA *is sitting on a chair, her head bowed.*
ROSEMARY *runs in, crouches on the floor. Draped over her head and
shoulders is the black and white cloth* LENA *made. Her body heaves as
she struggles for breath.*
WIRELESS *comes in.*
WIRELESS: (*To* ROSEMARY) But why did you stop dancing? (*He
draws beer from the drum, offers it to* ROSEMARY.)
You can drink all night. This beer won't harm you.
ROSEMARY: I'm hungry.
WIRELESS: Good. Hunger is good.
(ROSEMARY *runs to one side, retches, vomits.*
GAUDENCIA *goes to her.*
AMBUYA *dances in. She is dressed in a long black and white
dress trimmed with ribbons.*
WIRELESS *crouches and claps in greeting to* AMBUYA.)
Grandfather, you have come. Grandfather, you are welcome.
(AMBUYA *draws beer from the drum, drinks, then goes on
dancing quietly to one side.*)
(*To* ROSEMARY) That's good. Make your body empty. Then
fill it with beer.
(ROSEMARY *pulls off the black and white cloth.*)
ROSEMARY: I can't do it. Please!
GAUDENCIA: She's exhausted.
(LENA *runs in, crouches, wails in a deep voice.*)
WIRELESS: (*To* ROSEMARY) Watch her! She's fighting. Don't
fight! That's why she's in pain.
(*He crouches and claps to* LENA.)
Old woman, why do you hurt my wife? (*To* ROSEMARY) It's
her mother's grandmother. (*To* LENA) Be gentle with her.
Everyone has come to greet you, from the east, from the

west, from the village, from the bush. We're asking all the old ones: solve the problems of this house. Do you think we don't welcome you? We do!

(LENA *cries out in her own voice.*)

Lena? Or who?

LENA: Me.

WIRELESS: Dance. She'll come again.

LENA: I'm going home. I want to sleep.

(WIRELESS *draws beer, holds it to her mouth, forces her to drink.*)

WIRELESS: Dance! You want to. She'll come!

(LENA *starts to dance again. She and* AMBUYA *dance quietly together.*)

Forward with the old ones! I'm chairman of this business. I've got work to do.

(*He goes out.*

After a moment, JERICHO *comes in carrying a small box. He draws beer from the drum, drinks, spits it out.*)

JERICHO: Sour! Didn't I tell them: 'Wait until your maize is ripe?' No, I must hire a truck, push it up the mountain and half-way to town. The only grain I found was three years old. Stale grain won't make sweet beer.

(*He drinks, grimaces, drinks again.*

The drumming stops.

LENA *and* AMBUYA *rest.*)

I turn my back, they knock off. Damn those boys! I pay for them to play. (*To* ROSEMARY) Listen, this game of yours is costing me. Don't hide here. Dance! Let's go! Get out there!

(*He tries to pull* ROSEMARY *to her feet.*)

GAUDENCIA: Leave her.

JERICHO: In five hours she's hardly moved a foot. I must do something. There's not long to go.

GAUDENCIA: Your suffering's as great as hers. Don't punish her for that. If she won't dance maybe it should be you.

(*Silence.*)

JERICHO: I'll just run to the gate and check if anything's come up. When I'm back, if nothing's happened, I'll write the whole thing off as a bad job. (*To* ROSEMARY) Don't be cross.

I want you well, that's all. (*To* GAUDENCIA) Look after her
for me.
(*He goes.*
The drumming starts.
AMBUYA *dances over to* ROSEMARY, *gently raises her to her feet,*
dances round with her, pulls the cloth back over her head, then
dances out. ROSEMARY *dances out after her.*
LENA *is dancing quietly by herself.*
The drumming gets louder.
GAUDENCIA *draws beer, drinks, spits into her hand.*)
GAUDENCIA: It burns and comes up yellow. What does that
mean?
(SHUPI *comes in.*)
Poor girl. You're worn out. Sit with me.
SHUPI: I can't. She'll speak. I'll miss her.
(*She starts to go out.*)
GAUDENCIA: Are you ashamed of me? You think I betrayed you.
I did. What was I afraid of? Young men in suits? I was
elected chairman of this village, me a stranger, why? Because
of my courage in the war. I look at my clothes, I look at
theirs, I'm sorry, I can't speak.
(*The drumming stops.*
KINDO *runs in.*)
KINDO: (*To* SHUPI) Where is she?
SHUPI: Dancing.
KINDO: No. She's run off. Find her!
(SHUPI *runs out.*)
Her clothes are wet. Her forehead's white with salt. She's
shaking, crying. How can this be good?
(*He drinks.*
WIRELESS *comes in carrying a bowl.*)
(*To* WIRELESS) Your daughter's dead. You want to kill
mine!
(WIRELESS *ladles beer into the bowl.*)
WIRELESS: No, comrade. No, no, no. The old ones, what are
they actually? They're a committee. They're very wise
because they're very dead. They want us to be strong. And
why? They want beer. They can smell it on our breath. They

162

want drums. They hear them in our ears.
(*He gives the bowl to* KINDO.)
Drink.
(KINDO *drinks.*)
Drink!
(KINDO *drinks again.*)
Take it to the drummers. Go.
(KINDO *goes, taking the bowl.*)
I'm fighting hard. I'm shouting to my daughter: 'Don't
torture Rosemary for nothing! Make her feet jump! Get in!'
(AMBUYA *comes in, dances quietly.*)
And you?
GAUDENCIA: How can I dance here? This is not my home.
WIRELESS: These days the whole country's your home. Dance if
you want.
GAUDENCIA: I want. But it's up to him. If he wants he comes.
What can I do?
(WIRELESS *takes a bundle of clothes from under Gaudencia's
chair and unties it. It is a black and white dress. He lays it over
her.*
The drumming starts.
LENA *has been resting. Suddenly she leaps to her feet.*)
LENA: Oh, my brothers! Oh, my brothers! I am suffering! Aah!
Aah!
AMBUYA: (*To* LENA) Grandmother, you've come?
LENA: I'm here! I've come!
AMBUYA: Stamp your feet. Hard! Harder! Feel the pain.
LENA: I feel it.
AMBUYA: Pain is life.
LENA: Yes.
AMBUYA: Life is death.
LENA: Yes.
AMBUYA: Death is joy.
LENA: Yes.
AMBUYA: Joy is pain.
(LENA *stands panting and moaning.*
AMBUYA *claps her hand over* GAUDENCIA'*s mouth, holds it
there. When she releases it* GAUDENCIA *gasps for breath.*)

163

Breathe the air. Deep! Deeper! Is it sweet?

GAUDENCIA: It stinks! It's rotting!

AMBUYA: Good! Dance! She'll come.

(AMBUYA *and* LENA *moan, wail, dance round.*
LENA *dances out.*
GAUDENCIA *is wailing with pain.*)

GAUDENCIA: Ah! Ah! Ah! Ah!

WIRELESS: Come, grandmother. Come, put on your dress.

(WIRELESS *pulls the black and white dress over* GAUDENCIA'S
head.)

Your arm. Push through the hole. That's it. Now this one.
Please, grandmother.

GAUDENCIA: Oh, my brothers!

WIRELESS: Wait! The buttons!

(GAUDENCIA *gets up.*)

GAUDENCIA: Oh, my brothers!

(WIRELESS *picks up a ritual axe.*
GAUDENCIA *dances out.*)

WIRELESS: Wait! Your stick!

(*He runs out after her.*
The drumming gets louder.
ROSEMARY *dances in.* SHUPI *follows.*)

SHUPI: If you don't want to, don't. No one can force you. Come,
I'll take you home.

AMBUYA: Don't touch her! (*To* ROSEMARY) Come, my darling.
Come, my sweet one. Come, my strong, brave fighter.
Come.

(AMBUYA *lifts* ROSEMARY, *dances round with her. They both
dance out.*
Alone, SHUPI *tries to dance.*)

SHUPI: Freedom, she doesn't want you. She never did. I'm the
one who helped you, fought beside you. I want you. Come to
me.

(*She is still.*)

I can't do it. Is that why you don't want me?

(DANGER *comes in. He is wearing camouflage and carrying his
bag. He watches.*)

Make me dance. Come, Freedom. Come. Take me.

(*She sees* DANGER.)

Who are you?

DANGER: Comrade Danger. I've walked all day. I'll die if I don't
drink.

(SHUPI *gives him beer. He drinks.*)

Sorry about your leg. Was it the war?

(*Silence.*)

I'm asking how you were wounded.

SHUPI: I was shot. The day Freedom was killed.

DANGER: Comrade Freedom? Is that so? You knew her?

SHUPI: This was her home.

DANGER: Is that so? We were together maybe three, four years.

SHUPI: It's her they're trying to bring back.

DANGER: Is that so?

SHUPI: You think it's wrong?

DANGER: Some people say: 'What did we fight for?' To wake the
masses, to cleanse their minds of superstition. If that was it
we failed. Utterly. Everywhere I've been, all over the valley
they're drumming, drinking, bringing back the dead. On the
other hand, we also fought to give them back a sense of who
they are, their culture, history. For myself – I trained in
Finland, Cuba – it makes me uneasy.

(*He drinks.*)

SHUPI: If you didn't come to dance, what are you doing here?

DANGER: I'm searching for my mother. So far I've drawn a blank.
I'm glad to meet a friend of Freedom's. I better go.

(*The drumming gets louder.*

ROSEMARY *runs in wearing a black and white dress, waving a
ritual axe.*

GAUDENCIA, LENA *and* AMBUYA, *all possessed, all wearing
black and white, all waving ritual axes and sticks, dance in. The
dancing is now violent and warlike. The mediums dance and
whoop.*

WIRELESS *and* KINDO *run in and watch.*

The drumming stops.

The mediums are still.

WIRELESS *claps to the mediums.*)

WIRELESS: Welcome, grandmothers, grandfathers. We've got a

165

problem. Your grandchild is ill. Who sent this illness? That's what we want to know.

(*Silence*.)

DANGER: Oh god.

SHUPI: (*To* DANGER) What?

DANGER: Mother!

SHUPI: Sh!

WIRELESS: Who's that? (*To* DANGER) What's wrong, comrade?

DANGER: My mother. She's in pain.

WIRELESS: They're all our mothers and our fathers. I'm the chairman of this business. If you're quiet, you can stay here. If not, time to go.

(*The mediums seem exhausted. They shake themselves gently as though to free themselves from sleep.*

AMBUYA *groans*.)

Speak. We want to hear.

(*Silence*.)

ALL THE ANCESTORS: Aah! Aah! Aah! Ooh! Ooh! Ooh!

SHUPI: (*To* DANGER) Keep still.

DANGER: I've got to help her. Mother!

SHUPI: Sh!

DANGER: Then let me go.

WIRELESS: (*To* DANGER) Sit down!

(DANGER *does*.)

WIRELESS: Don't be angry, grandfathers. We're children. We know nothing. We can't live without you. Speak.

(*Silence.*

When the mediums speak they use voices deeper than their normal ones.)

AMBUYA: Are you –?

(*The ancestors laugh and make hooting noises.*)

WIRELESS: Grandfather?

(*Silence*.)

AMBUYA: Are you well?

WIRELESS: We are. Only our legs – haai! – from the dancing. And our heads – hoo! – from the drinking. That's how we are. And you?

AMBUYA: (*Wailing*) Oh, my brothers! It's dark. It's so dark!

166

KINDO: Must I light a lamp?
WIRELESS: They don't want lamps. It's your father's
    grandfather. Talk to him.
    (*Silence.*)
KINDO: Grandfather, of all my father's sons only I am living. I am
    dying now because of what is happening to this one, this
    daughter. I'll do anything to help her. Tell me.
AMBUYA: Water.
KINDO: He wants water.
    (WIRELESS *pours water into a cup and gives it to* AMBUYA.
    AMBUYA *takes water into her mouth, passes the cup to another
    medium, then sprays the water out of her mouth. In turn the other
    mediums do the same.*)
AMBUYA: (*Wailing*) You treat me so badly. Why? Oh oh oh oh.
    Why? You cry, cry, cry, complain, complain. How have I
    hurt you? How, my children? How?
DANGER: Mother, stop this. Mother, talk to me.
GAUDENCIA: (*Indicating* DANGER) That's the one! That's the one
    who's trying to kill us!
DANGER: What do you mean?
GAUDENCIA: They want to finish us!
WIRELESS: Who, Grandmother?
GAUDENCIA: The young ones like him.
WIRELESS: Who are they?
GAUDENCIA: They live – there! – on the mountain. They speak
    half-half. Half you can hear, half no one can understand.
    And they are proud. You must do what they say. But they do
    nothing. They want to finish us! They do!
    (*She throws herself at* DANGER, *hitting him.*
    WIRELESS *and* KINDO *pull her off him, settle her down.*)
DANGER: (*To* GAUDENCIA) Mother, don't you know me?
    (*Silence.*)
    JERICHO *runs in.*)
JERICHO: What the hell is going on? (*To* KINDO) Why didn't you
    call me?
KINDO: Throw him out! Don't let him in.
    (*The ancestors groan and wail.*)
    They want him out!

167

WIRELESS: If they want it, let them say so.

JERICHO: Who's in charge here?

WIRELESS: (*Of* AMBUYA) Him.

JERICHO: (*To* AMBUYA:) Grandfather, I'm her husband. Don't hear what they tell you. I love her, believe me. Help my wife.

AMBUYA: This one is not my blood.

JERICHO: What did he say?

AMBUYA: This one did not come out of my earth.

JERICHO: No, I was born on the mountain. But I paid for her. And I went to the shop and bought you beer.

(*The ancestors laugh.*)

AMBUYA: The beer is sour.

(*The ancestors laugh.*)

LENA: It's sour!

GAUDENCIA: It's sour!

AMBUYA: It's full of lumps. It's sour!

(*The ancestors laugh.*)

LENA: Is it brewed from maize we grew for you?

JERICHO: No. It's too early.

(*The ancestors laugh.*)

GAUDENCIA: You can't wait?

LENA: He can't wait!

(*The ancestors laugh.*)

JERICHO: We can't. She's ill.

(*He takes a black chicken from the box he has been carrying.*) I brought you this black chicken. I know you'd rather have a goat. All the goats round here were slaughtered by the soldiers. Please, take this instead.

(AMBUYA *takes the chicken.*)

AMBUYA: You think I've come to slaughter you?

DANGER: (*To* WIRELESS) What do I say?

WIRELESS: No.

JERICHO: No.

AMBUYA: Or to slaughter your wife?

WIRELESS: No.

JERICHO: No. But she hasn't eaten for a week. Who can live without food?

168

AMBUYA: Me!
 (*The ancestors laugh.*)
AMBUYA: ⎫
GAUDENCIA: ⎬Me! Me!
LENA: ⎭
 (*The ancestors laugh.*)
AMBUYA: She didn't eat. But did she die? No. Because I care for
    her. So why do you cry, cry, cry, cry, cry, cry, cry, cry, cry?
    She can speak if she wants. We're going. We've had enough
    of you.
 (*The men clap as they speak.*)
KINDO: Don't go! We need you!
WIRELESS: Grandfather, don't leave us.
JERICHO: Stay with us, Grandfather! Help us!
DANGER: I've had enough. I've got to go.
 (*Suddenly* ROSEMARY *begins to shake. She rolls on to the
 ground, cries out, rolls over and over hitting the ground violently
 with her arms.*
 *The mediums surround her, shaking themselves and hooting
 softly.*
 When they move aside, ROSEMARY *is sitting on the ground with
 the black and white cloth over her head.*
 Silence.
 When ROSEMARY *speaks, it is as if each word must be dragged
 up from the depths, as if each word causes pain.*
 She wails.
 WIRELESS *claps.*
 Silence.
 ROSEMARY *wails.*)
WIRELESS: What's your name?
ROSEMARY: Nedondo.
WIRELESS: Who?
 (*He claps.* KINDO *and* JERICHO *clap.*)
    Thank you, thank you for coming.
ROSEMARY: Oh, I am the country. Oh, I am the nation.
WIRELESS: Who are you?
ROSEMARY: Nedondo.
 (WIRELESS *claps.*)

169

WIRELESS: Welcome, Mother, welcome.

ROSEMARY: I live deep in this earth. Men walk over me, walk their boots over me. My face. My breasts. My thighs. Stick their steel spades into me. Dig me, drill me. Rip, tear my guts. Oh, my children. They hurt me. Me, Nedondo, mother of the country. Zimbabwe. Oh! Oh! Oh!

(*Silence. She laughs.*)

Let them dig deep. They can't reach me.

(*Silence.*)

WIRELESS: No. That's not the one. That one's trying to block the one who wants to speak.

(*He claps.* JERICHO *and* KINDO *clap.*

ROSEMARY *makes gutteral meaningless noises, falls silent.*

She tries again to speak, fails, falls silent.

She gets up, wanders round as though looking for something.

She finds DANGER. *At his feet is his bag. She opens it, takes out a camouflage jacket and cap, puts them on.*

Silence.

DANGER *and* ROSEMARY *look at each other.*)

DANGER: Who are you?

(*Silence.*)

Tell me.

(*Silence.*)

Comrade –

ROSEMARY: Ah! You know!

(*She laughs. The ancestors laugh.*)

DANGER: State your name distinctly. Do it.

(*Silence.*)

ROSEMARY: My name is Freedom. Comrade Freedom.

DANGER: Oh god. Bring me something to drink.

(WIRELESS *brings him beer. He drinks.*)

DANGER: Where are you?

(*Silence.*)

Precise co-ordinates of your position. Give them to me.

ROSEMARY: In the bush.

DANGER: I said precise.

ROSEMARY: Outside the village.

DANGER: Which one?

ROSEMARY: My father's.

DANGER: (*To* WIRELESS) I can't go on.

WIRELESS: Go on!

DANGER: (*To* ROSEMARY) You recognize these people?

ROSEMARY: I do.

DANGER: And you can trust them?

ROSEMARY: I can.

DANGER: You've got information for them?

ROSEMARY: I have.

DANGER: Good. Make your report.

(ROSEMARY *makes incoherent sounds.*

Silence.

ROSEMARY *makes incoherent sounds.*)

Comrade! Put your back straight. That's it! Be proud of who
you are. This is a debriefing. Tell us what you've got to say.
That's an instruction!

(*Silence.*)

Choppers overhead! Dive for cover!

(ROSEMARY *throws herself on to the ground.*)

All clear. No, there's another. Dive!

(ROSEMARY *does.*)

Good. Comrade, can you hear me?

ROSEMARY: Yes.

DANGER: Tell me what you want.

ROSEMARY: I want this country free.

DANGER: It is free!

ROSEMARY: I never saw it! I want to see it! This woman, this girl,
this Rosemary. I made her ill.

DANGER: Why?

ROSEMARY: Someone did something wrong.

DANGER: To who? To her?

ROSEMARY: To me.

DANGER: What did he do?

ROSEMARY: Betrayed me. This woman, this girl, this Rosemary
can't be well until he has admitted what he did.

DANGER: Who is it?

ROSEMARY: The one who betrayed me.

DANGER: Who was it?

ROSEMARY: Someone.

DANGER: This is an order. Tell me.

ROSEMARY: I've got other orders. I must go.

DANGER: Who did it? Freedom! Who betrayed you?

(*Silence.*)

WIRELESS: Please don't go, my daughter. Freedom! Stay with me.

AMBUYA: Fool! How can she?

(*It is dawn. The sky goes white. A deep red glow lights the faces of the mediums.*)

GAUDENCIA: The sun!

LENA: The sun!

AMBUYA: The sun!

(*The sun rises.*

One by one the mediums go. As they leave and the shadowy world of the mediums dissolves into the day-to-day world of the village, the tatters and tears in their black and white clothes can be seen.

SHUPI is fast asleep.

Kindo's bicycle is lying on the ground.

Mugs, cups, bowls, dishes are scattered round.

DANGER and JERICHO sit on the chairs.

WIRELESS and KINDO stretch, drink another mouthful of beer, wash their faces, rinse out their mouths with water, sit out in the sun.

LENA comes on in her everyday clothes.)

WIRELESS: (*To LENA*) You need some beer?

(*He gives her beer. She sits and drinks.*)

OK?

LENA: OK.

WIRELESS: (*To JERICHO*) Don't forget to pay the drummers.

(*JERICHO goes out.*

KINDO stretches, yawns, takes off his shoes, rubs his feet.)

(*To DANGER, of the beer*) There's plenty. You want some?

(*He gives beer to DANGER.*)

KINDO: (*To DANGER*) So you came back?

DANGER: I did.

(*AMBUYA comes on in her everyday clothes.*)

WIRELESS: Ah! There you are, Grandmother.

(AMBUYA *starts to tidy up the mugs and cups.*
WIRELESS *gives beer to* KINDO.)
The first time, they never tell you everything. Let her rest.
In a month or two we'll try again.
(GAUDENCIA *comes on in her everyday clothes. She sits next to*
LENA. *They whisper to each other.*
AMBUYA *goes over to* LENA *and* GAUDENCIA. *The three women*
laugh and whisper together.
JERICHO *comes on.*)
JERICHO: Who promised them so much? It wasn't me.
KINDO: (*To* DANGER) So who are you?
(DANGER *goes to* SHUPI, *wakes her.*)
SHUPI: Did she come?
DANGER: She did.
SHUPI: Why did no one wake me? Did she speak?
DANGER: She did.
SHUPI: What did she say?
DANGER: Someone betrayed her.
KINDO: (*To* WIRELESS) Let's go to the river. I want to wash my
    feet.
SHUPI: Who?
(ROSEMARY *comes on in her everyday clothes. She sits.*
LENA, AMBUYA *and* GAUDENCIA *fall silent.*
Silence.
The three women start whispering again.)
Who betrayed Freedom? Does anybody know? If you want
Rosemary to get well, you have to say.
(*Silence.*)
WIRELESS: She was in the bush, I don't know where. She came
    into my house. She had a gun, this big. She asked me will I
    take it to someone on the mountain. I said: 'No. If they catch
    me, they'll kill me. Why not you?' She said: 'It's urgent. I
    can't go by bus, the soldiers know me.' She's my daughter.
    What could I do? At night I crept into his house, took his
    bike, gave it to her. He says he gave it to guerrillas. He'd
    rather give his teeth. She's gone. Next thing, soldiers!
    'Comrades were here!' 'No, baas.' 'Don't lie to me!' Whaa!
    Whaa! I'm bleeding, my nose broken. 'Yes, baas, yes, there

was. They went into the bush.' Whaa! Whaa! I'm on the
floor. 'Don't lie! Who was here?' 'My daughter, baas.' Don't
blame me. I had to save my life. 'Where did she go?' 'There.
Up the mountain.' 'With others?' 'No, alone.' 'On foot? By
bus?' (*Silence*.) 'On a bike.' (*He is crying*.) Who betrayed her?
Me.

(*Silence*.)

JERICHO:Any car, bus, bicycle that passes through the gate must
first be sprayed by me. All I said to her was: 'Why not take
your parcel off the carrier? I don't want to wet it with my
spray.' She shot off down the road, round the gate, up the
mountain. I can't make exceptions. Every cow in the land
will die of sleeping disease. Then I saw there were jeeps after
her. I shouted: 'Someone's taking tsetse up the mountain.'
The jeeps were off. We saw her in the headlights. She knew
she couldn't get away. She turned, sped back so fast they
kept on missing her. I could have closed the gate when she'd
gone through. A jeep can knock it flat. Could I have saved
her? I didn't even try. It's no surprise she's so angry with
me.

(*Silence*.)

KINDO: They said no one may touch her. There she lies, bullets in
her brain, there she must rot. I thought: if they're so cruel
they can kill a young girl, how can we ever win? I thought,
the government will still be here when the war is over.
They're going to need a headman. I know the people. It
might as well be me. I went at night. I prised open her legs,
her elbows. The bones in her hands cracked. I pulled my
bike out, wheeled it home. The one she hates, the reason that
she wants to kill my daughter – me.

(*Silence*.)

ROSEMARY: You pulled the bike from her. That's what I saw.

KINDO: You saw?

ROSEMARY: I did.

KINDO: That's why you ran away?

(GAUDENCIA *has been watching* DANGER.)

DANGER: The person waiting for the gun Freedom was bringing
up the mountain – it was me. I waited for it. It never came.

174

So I was caught and beaten up and tried and put in jail. After the war I lay in hospital. Mother, that is where I've been.

GAUDENCIA: I thought the sun was up.

DANGER: It is.

GAUDENCIA: What world is this where the dead walk after dawn? Or is the dead one me?
(*She feels him gently.*)
You're Herbert?

DANGER: In the war I was Danger. If I'm Herbert it must be peace.
(GAUDENCIA *starts to dance.*
ROSEMARY *has been watching* GAUDENCIA *and* DANGER. *Now she starts to cry. She cries and cries.*
SHUPI *goes to comfort her.*
AMBUYA *is comforting* KINDO. WIRELESS *and* LENA *are sitting together.*
GAUDENCIA *stops dancing, sits with* DANGER.)

JERICHO: So what happens now? Is Freedom at rest?
(ROSEMARY *stops crying, recovers.*)

ROSEMARY: I feel better.

JERICHO: Good. Are you coming with me?
(ROSEMARY *shakes her head.*)
I said it was a waste of cash. She's no better than she was. See what I mean?

ROSEMARY: (*To* WIRELESS *and* LENA) You got her back, then I took her away. At least you've got each other. (*To* KINDO) What can I do for you?
(*She wanders over to Kindo's bicycle, runs her fingers over it.*)
The truth is – what I feel is – I'm so damn hungry.

LENA: Me as well.

GAUDENCIA: Me too.

DANGER: Of course. Your rations didn't come. Blame your foolish chairman. Where is she?
(*Silence.*)

GAUDENCIA: I'm here.

DANGER: I mean the chairman of this village. Mother, is it you?
(*Everyone laughs, except* ROSEMARY. *They laugh and laugh.*
ROSEMARY *has lifted up the bicycle. Now she gets on it and rides round.*

Everyone watches her in silence.
ROSEMARY *stops*.)

ROSEMARY: When I ran away, I went up the mountain. It's time I
went again. I'll go to the District Office. I'll get our food. I
won't be afraid of anyone. (*To* KINDO) Don't worry about
your bike. I'll bring it back.

KINDO: My daughter, I give it to you.
(ROSEMARY *rides round*.)

GAUDENCIA: Forward with the year of reconciliation!

ALL: Forward!

GAUDENCIA: Forward with the struggle of the people!

ALL: Forward!
(ROSEMARY *rides out*.
They watch her go.)

SHUPI: Freedom, keep going! Keep going, Rosemary!